Iran

Iran

The Essential Guide to a
Country on the Brink

ENCYCLOPÆDIA
Britannica®

Encyclopædia Britannica

WILEY

John Wiley & Sons, Inc.

Photo credits: page 70: Bettmann/Corbis; page 77: Françoise de Mulder/Corbis; page 81: United States Department of Defense/Petty Officer 1st Class Brien Aho, U.S. Navy; page 83: United States Department of Defense/Airman 1st Class Kurt Gibbons III, U.S. Air Force; page 85: United States Department of Defense/Specialist Katherine M. Roth/U.S. Army; page 113: © Raheb Homavandi—Reuters/Corbis; page 115: Morteza Nikoubazl—Reuters/Corbis; pages 119, 126: Credit AFP/Getty Images; page 128: Alain Keler/Sygma; page 131: UPI/Compix/EB Inc.; page 134: Fred J. Maroon—Photo Researchers; page 21: © Mohsen Shandiz/Corbis; page 164: Keystone; page 191: Kaveh Kazemi/Corbis; page 193: Robert Harding Picture Library; page 214: Ray Manley; Shostal Assoc./EB Inc; page 216: Robert Harding Picture Library/Sybil Sassoon; page 219: By courtesy of the Oriental Institute, the University of Chicago.

Published by John Wiley & Sons, Inc., Hoboken, New Jersey
Published simultaneously in Canada

Design and composition by Navta Associates, Inc.

For general information about our other products and services, please contact our Customer Care Department within the United States at (800) 762-2974, outside the United States at (317) 572-3993 or fax (317) 572-4002.

Wiley also publishes its books in a variety of electronic formats. Some content that appears in print may not be available in electronic books. For more information about Wiley products, visit our web site at www.wiley.com.

Library of Congress Cataloging-in-Publication Data:

Iran : the essential guide to a country on the brink / Encyclopædia Britannica.
    p. cm.
  Includes bibliographical references.
  ISBN-13 978-0-471-74151-5 (pbk.)
  ISBN-10 0-471-74151-0 (pbk.)
  1. Iran. I. Encyclopædia Britannica, inc.
  DS254.5.I748 2005
  955.05—dc22

Printed in the United States of America

10 9 8 7 6 5 4 3 2 1

Contents

53 - 54

Iran

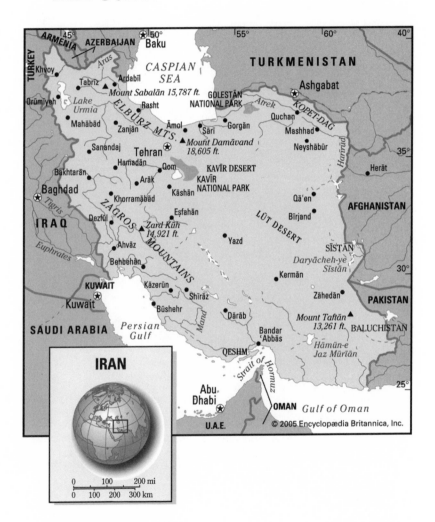

ARMENIA · AZERBAIJAN · Baku · 45° · 50° · 55° · 60° · 40° · TURKMENISTAN

TURKEY · Khvoy · Tabrīz · Ardabīl · *Aras* · Mount Sabalān 15,787 ft. · CASPIAN SEA · Ashgabat

Orūmīyeh · *Lake Urmia* · Rasht · GOLESTĀN NATIONAL PARK · *Atrek* · Quchan · KOPET-DAG

Mahābād · Zanjān · Āmol · Sārī · Gorgān · Mashhad · 35°

Sanandaj · Tehran ⊛ · Mount Damāvand 18,605 ft. · Neyshābūr · Herāt

Bakhtarān · Hamadān · Qom · KAVĪR DESERT · Qā'en · AFGHANISTAN

Baghdad ⊛ · Arāk · Kāshān · KAVĪR NATIONAL PARK

Tigris · Khorramābād · Eşfahān · Bīrjand

IRAQ · Dezfūl · *Zard Kūh 14,921 ft.* · LŪT DESERT

Euphrates · Ahvāz · Yazd · SĪSTĀN · 30°

Behbehān · *Daryācheh-ye Sīstān*

KUWAIT · Kāzerūn · Kermān · Zāhedān · PAKISTAN

Kuwait ⊛ · Būshehr · Shīrāz · Dārāb · Mount Taftān 13,261 ft. · BALUCHISTAN

SAUDI ARABIA · *Persian Gulf* · *Mand* · Bandar 'Abbās · *Hāmūn-e Jaz Mūrīān*

QESHM · *Strait of Hormuz* · 25°

Abu Dhabi ⊛ · OMAN · *Gulf of Oman*

U.A.E. · © 2005 Encyclopædia Britannica, Inc.

IRAN

0 · 100 · 200 mi
0 · 100 · 200 · 300 km

Note to the Reader

Encyclopædia Britannica is one of the most trusted sources of information around the globe. Its 44-million-word encyclopaedia is often cited as the most authoritative reference work in the world, and its 32-volume print set, first published in 1768, is the oldest continuously published and revised work in the English language. And so it is with great pleasure that we offer today, in conjunction with John Wiley & Sons, yet another way to access Britannica's wealth of information: the "Essential Guide" series.

The first volume in this series, *Iran: The Essential Guide to a Country on the Brink*, looks at a key country in the Middle East, one at the center of great controversy concerning its relations with its neighbors, its interest in nuclear power, and its purported role in what President George W. Bush has called an "axis of evil." Iran's people, culture, resources, and politics are all examined in the concise but informative entries that follow.

The entries derive from *Encyclopædia Britannica*'s extensive coverage of Iran and Persian history, and they are arranged alphabetically for easy access to specific subjects. But many readers will doubtless choose to read this book straight through, from beginning to end, and we've developed the entries with this in mind. So whether you choose to skip around or to read this book cover to cover, we trust you'll find the information and explanations you're looking for.

To help put these entries in the context of contemporary world affairs, we've supplemented them with contributions from several noted writers. For example, Stephen Kinzer, longtime correspondent for the *New York Times* and author of *All the Shah's Men: An American Coup and the Roots of Middle East Terror*, has written the introduction to the book. He surveys the state of Iranian politics and wonders what it will take to see a reconciliation between Iran and the United States. There are also special sidebar essays, such as Strobe Talbott's "Bush, Iraq, and the World." Talbott, a former journalist for *Time* and U.S. deputy secretary of state and now president of the Brookings Institution in Washington, D.C., highlights the U.S. "war on terrorism" and America's military operations in Iraq, Iran's neighbor to the west.

The combination of these various article types, all arranged in this easy-to-use format, should provide you with a quick, concise, and informative introduction to this important (but often puzzling) country in the Middle East. And if more detailed information on any aspect of Iran is desired, there are additional sources listed in a bibliography at the end of this book. We also invite you to visit www.britannica.com, where authoritative answers are always just a click away.

Theodore Pappas
Executive Editor
Encyclopædia Britannica, Inc.

Introduction

Steven Kinzer

One spring afternoon in 1997, the telephone at the *New York Times* bureau in Istanbul rang. I was then serving as bureau chief, and the caller was my boss, the *Times* foreign editor. An election was soon to be held in Iran, he said, and he had chosen me to cover it.

"Get yourself a visa," he told me, "buy a plane ticket, go to Iran, and then tell us what's really happening there."

Trying to find out what is really happening in Iran has been a challenge to outsiders for centuries. This is a country whose history stretches back over millennia, one that has known both the heights of world power and the depths of poverty and isolation. In its modern incarnation, it puzzles outsiders as much as ever. Its people seem to embrace tradition while they thirst for modernity. Their society appears both terribly repressive and vibrantly democratic. Iranian leaders have done much to stabilize and pacify the Middle East, but at least as much to destabilize and try to dominate it. These contradictions, along with Iran's enormous potential to influence the course of world events, make it one of the world's most fascinating countries.

In the weeks leading up to the 1997 election, I traveled across Iran and spoke to hundreds of people, ranging from government ministers to illiterate peasants. Like almost everyone who visits there, I stopped at places that evoke the country's rich history, from the haunting ruins of Persepolis, the former royal capital that Alexander the Great sacked in 330 BC, to the spectacular mosques and palaces of Esfahan. Everywhere I found Iranians torn between hope and fear, wanting to believe that their country could once again rise to greatness but deeply uncertain that it could.

The election campaign perfectly reflected these competing impulses. One candidate was a colorless bureaucrat who had been handpicked by the ruling elite. One of his opponents, Mohammad Khatami, a former minister of culture who had lived abroad and liked to quote Western philosophers, was all but unknown, and seemed for most of the campaign to be nothing more than a sacrificial lamb offered up for electoral slaughter. Then, less than two weeks before the vote, something happened that no one had expected. Khatami caught the imagination of his people. He told them Iran needed to change, open its society, and launch a "dialogue of civilizations" with the rest of the world. In the last days of his campaign, as defenders of the old order watched in dismay, he took on rock-star popularity, thronged wherever he went by admirers who chanted his name. He won the presidency in a landslide victory, taking 69 percent of the vote.

The day after the election, I wandered the streets of Tehran and found people giddy with joy and disbelief. All knew they had scored a great triumph over the dour regime many of them detested, but few dared to guess what their defiance might mean. In a small antiques store, I found the proprietor engaged in an animated argument with his nephew, who was also his shop assistant.

"This was a referendum about freedom," the older man insisted. "The voters were saying that we're tired of people snooping into our private lives. What we do at home is our own business. With Khatami in power, the government is going to stop telling us what we can read, what we can watch, and what we can do. We voted for change, and the government will have to give it to us."

From behind the counter, his nephew smiled and shook his head in gentle disagreement. "Khatami is not the boss and never will be," he said. "In this country the president does not decide. Maybe Khatami has certain ideas, but he won't have real power."

The debate in that shop crystallized the conflict that shapes modern Iran, and also the outside world's uncertainty about what Iran is and what it can become. Iran is a large and very proud country, acutely conscious of its rich heritage and unwilling to accept dictates from any outside power. It is also insecure and confused, its people deeply divided over what kind of society they want at home and what role they should play in the world. Iran may emerge from this conundrum as an outlaw nation, one that thumbs its nose at the world and pushes toward dangerous confrontations with other powerful states and groups of states. It also, however, can become an example of democracy and stability in a region that has known precious little of either. It is this dichotomy, this contradiction, this remarkable potential to shape the Middle East and the wider world for better or worse, that makes Iran as important as it is fascinating. The purpose of this book, like others in the Britannica series, is to provide serious but easily digestible insights on such subjects as Iran, subjects that interest people around the world.

Many countries in today's Middle East are modern creations. Their borders come not from nature or history, but from the whims of colonialists who met at men's clubs in European capitals to draw lines on maps. That is why it is difficult, for example, to describe a "true" Jordanian tradition or Saudi Arabian heritage or Iraqi consciousness. Just the opposite is the case with Iran. This is one of the world's oldest and most self-confident nations. In the minds of its people, they have spoken more or less the same language and lived within more or less the same boundaries for thousands of years. They have a very strong sense of themselves and their rich traditions. They feel insulted when younger countries such as the United States, which is powerfully armed but sometimes weak in historical understanding, try to tell them what to do.

The king who unified Persia in the sixth century BC, Cyrus the Great, captured some of his domain by war but brought other princes into his realm by negotiation. He was also famous for his declared toleration for conquered peoples, rather than oppressing them, and for freeing the Hebrew captives in

Babylonia and allowing them to return to their homeland. So this land, although it has lived through periods of obscurantism and repression, was also one of the first to recognize the importance of tolerance and diversity. The Iranian lawyer Shirin Ebadi made a point of embracing this heritage in her speech accepting the Nobel Peace Prize in 2003. She called herself "a descendant of Cyrus the Great, the very emperor who proclaimed at the pinnacle of power 2,500 years ago that he 'would not reign over the people if they did not wish it.'"

Cyrus and his successors built an empire that stretched from Greece, across modern-day Turkey and Lebanon, through the North African provinces of Libya and Egypt, and all the way to the banks of the Indus. It suffered a great defeat when Alexander broke into the Persian homeland and devastated Persepolis, but since then it has enjoyed several periods of prosperity, influence, and cultural innovation.

A profound change came to Persia in the seventh century, when Arab invaders swept through the land and captured it. With them they brought their religion, Islam, and over a period of generations, nearly all Persians accepted it. The brand of Islam most Iranians now profess, called Shi'ism, seems to them the truest form. Some Sunni Muslim fanatics such as Osama bin Laden, however, still consider it a form of apostasy and do not consider Shi'ites to be truly formed Muslims.

In the beginning, the split between Sunni and Shi'ite Islam was bloody and painful. Both of the revered founders of the Shi'ite tradition, Ali and Hussein, were martyred. According to legend, Hussein continued to chant the Qur'an even after his head was severed. This heritage has given Shi'ites a collective sense of pain and, in times of crisis, a thirst to emulate the martyrdom of their forefathers.

Under Iran's first Shi'ite dynasty, the Safavids, who came to power in 1501, Persia reached a pinnacle of world power. The Safavids turned Esfahan into a bustling center of world trade and culture, but also ruled with a brutality that was shocking even by the standards of that era. They symbolized what one modern author has called "the peculiar mixture of cruelty and liberalism, barbarity and sophistication, magnificence and voluptuousness, that made up Persian civilization."

The Safavids held power for about two centuries, finally collapsing in the face of an invasion from Afghanistan in 1722. Later the country came under the rule of a corrupt and dissipated clan, the Qajars, whose incompetence reduced Persia to a state of misery and subservience to foreign powers. As the Qajar Dynasty fell into its death throes in the late nineteenth century, it was challenged not by another feudal clan, but by a force that was new in Iran: democracy. A reform-minded mix of modern Iranian intellectuals and traditional elites built a powerful mass movement that culminated in the epochal Constitutional Revolution of 1905.

Ever since then, Iranians have thirsted for democracy. They have had more of it than almost any of their neighbors, but not nearly enough to satisfy them. For twenty years beginning in 1921, they were ruled by a soldier turned emperor who from 1925 called himself Reza Shah Pahlavi. He reinvigorated a nation that was on the edge of extinction, but tolerated no dissent and showed his critics little mercy.

After World War II, Iranians propelled a visionary leader who embraced the true essence of democracy, Mohammad Mossadeq, to power. Mossadeq's greatest achievement was the nationalization of the country's oil industry, which had been controlled by a singularly powerful British monopoly, the Anglo-Iranian Oil Company. That daring act made him a national hero and assured him a place in Iranian history, but it also led to his downfall. In 1953, outraged by Mossadeq's challenge to their power, the British, working closely with the CIA, arranged to overthrow him. That opened a new era in Iranian history, one dominated by Reza Shah's son, Mohammad Reza Shah Pahlavi, who ruled with increasing repression until he was himself overthrown in the Islamic Revolution of 1978–1979.

The new regime brought a revolutionary Islamic government to power, and they proved to be hostile to the United

Sates. In an act that shocked the world, this regime allowed radical students to take 66 American diplomats hostage and hold them captive for more than 14 months. That act helped destroy the presidency of Jimmy Carter and turned Washington and Tehran into bitter enemies. From that moment, each has seized every chance to hurt the other, as when the United States provided aid to Iran's bitter enemy Saddam Hussein during the horrific Iran-Iraq War in the 1980s.

The United States has used a host of tools to weaken Iran. It has encouraged Iranian revolutionary groups, imposed economic sanctions on Iran, and worked intensely to prevent Iran from building pipelines that could carry its oil and gas to nearby countries. This pressure intensified after President George W. Bush took office in 2001. Bush famously listed Iran, along with Iraq and North Korea, as part of the world's "axis of evil" and claimed in his second inaugural address that Iran had become "the world's primary state sponsor of terror." Vice President Dick Cheney asserted that "Iran is at the top of the list" of world trouble spots. Secretary of State Condoleezza Rice called Iran's human rights record "a thing to be loathed." All said they hoped diplomacy would find a solution to problems between the two countries, but many seemed to consider it a dead end.

Some American policymakers believe that the United States should not engage with Iran because it makes no sense to negotiate with a regime one wishes to destroy—or at least hopes will soon collapse. Americans are also put off by Iran's record of sponsoring terrorism around the world. Iranian agents, acting with the support of at least some factions in the regime, have assassinated dissident exiles in various European capitals; launched attacks on American military bases; and even, according to several intelligence agencies, planned the 1994 bombing of a Jewish community center in Buenos Aires that took 85 lives. The regime appears to have pulled back from this murderous course but has not offered the credible assurances necessary if it expects to be treated as a member in good standing of the world community. It still supports groups such as Hezbollah in Lebanon that militantly oppose the faltering Middle East peace process, yet even this seems open to negotiation. Resolving the Israeli-Palestinian dispute is seen by many as an absolute prerequisite to stability in the Middle East, and although Iran has been no friend of the peace process, its very militancy could make it a uniquely valuable force if it could be enticed to moderate its position.

Today, Iran is in the grip of a repressive regime. Some of its leaders seem to hate not only the West, but also the very ideas of progress and modernity. Yet this regime is no conventional tyranny, any more than Iranians are docile subjects who can be easily repressed. For much of the past 10 years, Iran has been ruled by what amount to two governments. One is a functioning democracy, complete with elections, a feisty press, and a cadre of reformist politicians. The other is a narrow-minded clique of conservatives, comprised largely of mullahs, that has in many ways lost touch with the masses and sometimes seems to have no agenda other than closing newspapers and blocking democratic change.

Outsiders may be forgiven for seeing Iran as a country that can never make up its mind. Should it punish prison guards who abuse dissidents, or reward them? Should it cooperate with foreigners who want to monitor its nuclear program, or defy them? Should it allow reformers to run for Parliament, or ban them? Iranian officials seem to contradict themselves endlessly on these and countless other questions, changing their positions from one day to the next. Behind their apparent indecision is a constant struggle among various factions, ranging from an Islamist old guard to democratic insurgents who want to open Iran to the broader world. One group is dominant for a while, then another becomes stronger.

Khatami's presidency, which lasted from 1997 to 2005, proved to be a huge disappointment for many Iranians. Although Khatami never renounced his reformist principles, he seemed unwilling to fight for them and appeared to succumb to pressure from reactionary clerics who viewed, and still view, every cry for change as the germ of a frightful disease that must be stamped out before it can infect the nation. When Khatami appeared before students at Tehran University in the last year of his presidency, they interrupted his speech with angry chants of "Shame on you!" and "Where are your promised freedoms?"

Despite Khatami's evident failures, however, he shifted the center of political gravity in his country. He showed the world that Iran has a strong majority that wants change. His presidency also made clear that Iran is not a closed garrison state like North Korea, and that its clerical regime is not a self-destructive dictatorship like the one Saddam Hussein imposed on Iraq. Its leaders, including the reactionary mullahs, are eminently rational. Political and social ideas are more freely debated in Iran now than at any time since the Mossadeq era.

The election of 2005, held to choose a successor to President Khatami, seemed to tip Iran's political balance strongly toward the more conservative faction. Mahmoud Amadinejad, the former mayor of Tehran aligned with the mullahs, won after the Council of Guardians refused to allow most reformist candidates to run. He has a history of collaborating with groups that have used every means, including violence, to maintain the religious purity of the Islamic regime. He also raised the stakes in his country's confrontation with the West over Iran's nuclear program. By the time he took office, fears over this program had become the central issue in Iran's troubled relationship with the outside world.

Although Iranian officials insist that their nuclear program has only peaceful purposes, outsiders may be forgiven for suspecting that its true purpose is to produce atomic weapons. Seen from the Iranian perspective, this would make perfect sense. Israel, a likely adversary in any future conflict, has nuclear weapons. So does the United States, which has troops on both Iran's western border (in Iraq) and its eastern border (in Afghanistan). Even India and Pakistan, two midlevel powers with which Iran compares itself, have nuclear arsenals. It is not difficult to see how Iranians can conclude that their security interests require them to acquire such weapons as well.

To foreign powers, however, and especially to the United States, the prospect of a nuclear-armed Iran is horrific and intolerable. It is uncertain whether Iran's Islamic regime is today supporting terrorist groups, but it clearly did so as recently as the 1990s. It harbors, as it has always harbored, a desire to be a dominant power in the Middle East and Central Asia. These facts, combined with the Shi'ite belief in self-sacrifice and martyrdom, have led many world leaders to conclude that Iran must be prevented from entering the nuclear club. This conflict could spiral into world crisis.

One suggested way to head off this crisis might be for world powers, particularly the United States, to strike a "grand bargain" with Iran. As envisioned by some European leaders, this might include new security guarantees for Iran, an end to economic sanctions and other measures that have isolated it from much of the world, and a variety of other concessions in exchange for a verifiable pledge that Iran would not develop nuclear weapons. European leaders have tried to negotiate such a bargain but have been conspicuously unsuccessful. Only the United States can offer Iran what it wants: a guarantee that it will not be attacked and will, instead, be treated as a normal member of the world community.

At various times in the modern era, American leaders have negotiated with oppressive regimes, including some that have perpetrated crimes far worse than any the Iranian mullahs have committed. Iran and the United States have even negotiated with one another when it seemed in their best interests to do so, as they did during the Iran-Contra Affair discussed in this volume. Iran, however, remains one of the few countries that the United States seems to consider beyond the political pale, one that is to be warned and threatened but never invited to the table for serious bargaining

The Islamic Revolution of 1978–1979 was a huge shock to the United States, one from which it has never fully recovered.

Iran was a secure source of oil, a huge market for American weaponry, and a base from which the United States projected power throughout the Middle East and beyond. Militants who seized power there after the revolution seethed with hatred of the United States, which they blamed for destroying their democracy in 1953 and supporting the autocratic Mohammad Reza Shah Pahlavi for 25 years. They showed their anger by taking American diplomats hostage and, according to American intelligence reports, sponsoring attacks against U.S. military targets in Lebanon, Saudi Arabia, and elsewhere. These events left Americans feeling deeply wronged. Many believe the Iranian regime has escaped the punishment it deserves. They are still looking for a way to inflict it. The idea of negotiating with a regime they consider responsible for heinous acts of terror is abhorrent to them.

This impulse is in sharp contrast to the respectful relationship the United States has built with Vietnam, the other country that dealt a devastating blow to the United States during the 1970s. In dealing with Vietnam, American officials decided to forget old grievances and work together toward common goals. They have not done that in their dealings with Iran. That may be because many Americans have come to conclude that their war in Vietnam was ill-conceived. They have reached no such conclusion about Iran.

Whether serious negotiations between Washington and Tehran would produce a breakthrough is far from certain. Hard-liners in both capitals would certainly try to undermine them. Besides, Iran is now in less of a mood to compromise than it might have been in past years. That is partly because the election of President Amadinejad has consolidated the power of militants who reject the idea of negotiation with the United States. The changing world situation, however, has also greatly encouraged Iranian leaders. Iran has built good relations with India, China, and Russia, all of whom want to buy Iranian oil and natural gas, so Iran no longer feels as isolated as it did in the 1990s. It also sees the Middle East balance tilting in its favor as a result of the American invasion and occupation of Iraq.

Iranian leaders view Operation Iraqi Freedom as enormously favorable to their interests. It led to the downfall of Saddam Hussein, Iran's bitterest enemy in the Middle East; pinned down so many American troops that hardly any remain for a possible strike against Iran; and isolated the United States in the court of world opinion. In Shi'ite regions of Iraq, it left a power vacuum that Iran rushed to fill.

"Throughout Iraq," a senior Iranian intelligence officer gloated two years after the American invasion, "the people we supported are in power."

His jubilation was understandable. Iranian intelligence services worked for decades to build their influence in Iraq, but had little success until the United States gave them the chance. Now southern Iraq, which under the new Iraqi constitution is a semiautonomous region, has shifted politically closer to Iran. It is no surprise that many Iranian strategists believe their country has emerged as the real winner of Operation Iraqi Freedom.

Iran has the human and natural resources to be at least as successful as regional powers such as Brazil, Turkey, and South Africa, but Iran's people suffer under a regime whose failures have given them only a marginally democratic political system and a plethora of social ills. Many find escape in a burgeoning subculture that revolves around the Internet, satellite television, and other subversive tools, but they shy away from political protest. They remember that in the late 1970s, they rebelled against a repressive regime, only to find themselves with one that was, in many ways, even worse. That has taught them that it is wiser to allow political events to take their course than to rebel in ways that may only increase their unhappiness.

Although today's Iran poses a clear threat to world order, it also holds out tantalizing possibilities. The Islamic revolutionaries appear deeply unpopular. A huge population of young people—two-thirds of Iranians are under 35—is literate, educated, and eager for democratic change. And unlike most of their neighbors, Iranians share a collective experience of more than a century of struggle for democracy, as well as a fervent wish for true freedom. Many find inspiration in their history.

Given this history of mutual distrust between Iran and the United States, what are the prospects for reconciliation? Leaders of both countries are deeply convinced their cause is righteous, even to the extent of believing that God is on their side. That makes this a particularly difficult conflict to resolve.

Part of this is due to a clash of perceptions. The United States is the world's dominant power, and has assumed the right not only to judge other nations but also to punish those it considers "rogue states." From Washington, Iran looks like many other Third World countries that are ruled by tyrants but are susceptible to one or another form of American pressure. Iranians see the world quite differently. Their country has existed for thousands of years and has made enormous contributions to world culture. Like other ancient nations, it has risen and fallen time and again. Its leaders find it ludicrous that the United States, which they see as an arrogant new country already entering into a period of decline, should presume to lecture them about anything. Until these perceptions come a bit closer to each other, the prospects for reconciliation will remain dim.

Twenty-five years of bitter hostility between Iran and the United States might seem to suggest that these countries, at least under their present forms of government, are destined to stay enemies. Beneath the angry surface of their relationship, however, they have many interests in common. Both are wary of the power and intentions of Sunni Arab states. Both detest radical Sunni movements such as the Taliban and al-Qaeda. Iran also has vast reserves of oil, the commodity Americans consume more voraciously than anyone else on Earth. Far from being natural enemies, these two countries are potential allies.

This is no longer a marginal view. In 2004 a task force sponsored by the Council on Foreign Relations in New York, and chaired by two pillars of the American foreign policy establishment, former CIA director Robert Gates and former national security adviser Zbigniew Brzezinski, recommended "a revised strategic approach to Iran."

"It is in the interests of the United States to engage selectively with Iran to promote regional stability, dissuade Iran from pursuing nuclear weapons, preserve reliable energy supplies, reduce the threat of terror, and address the 'democracy deficit' that pervades the Middle East," they wrote. "A basic statement of principles, along the lines of the 1972 Shanghai Communiqué signed by the United States and China, could be developed to outline the parameters for U.S.-Iranian engagement, establish the overarching objectives for dialogue, and reassure relevant domestic political constituencies on both sides."

As Iran presses ahead with its nuclear program, it is on the brink of a potentially deadly confrontation with the outside world. The militancy of many of its leaders, and that of many of their counterparts in Washington, has sharply reduced the prospects for compromise. Without such a compromise, however, Iran may find itself at the center of a global crisis. That makes it more important than ever for the outside world to understand this ancient land.

Stephen Kinzer, a longtime foreign correspondent for the New York Times, *has reported from more than fifty countries on four continents. He is the author of the national best seller* All the Shah's Men: An American Coup and the Roots of Middle East Terror.

Afghanistan: "Operation Enduring Freedom"

Within days of the September 11 attacks on the United States, NATO, for the first time in its history, invoked Article 5 of its charter, declaring that the atrocities were an attack on the alliance. As a demonstration of support, Australia invoked the Australia–New Zealand–United States (ANZUS) Treaty, putting elements of its armed forces on a higher state of readiness in case they were called upon to assist the United States. On September 19 the Organization of American States agreed by acclamation to invoke the Rio Treaty, also a mutual-defense pact.

Although the Iranian leadership, notably President Mohammad Khatami, was quick to condemn the September 11 attacks, hopes that the campaign against terrorism would offer some degree of rapprochement between the United States and Iran were dimmed in late September when the Iranian spiritual leader (*rahbar*), Ali Khamenei, made a severely anti-American speech in which he explicitly rejected, except under a UN banner, Iranian participation in any actions against the Taliban government in Afghanistan—which sheltered al-Qaeda, the perpetrators of the September 11 attacks—or in a global anti-terrorist movement.

The country that sheltered the Islamic militants who perpetrated the September 11 attacks was one laid waste by more than 20 years of unremitting warfare. From 1978, forces of Afghanistan's Communist government battled Islamic guerrillas for control of the country and were assisted by Soviet troops from 1979 to 1989. Mujahideen guerrillas were themselves supported by the United States—who saw aid for the guerrillas as a risk-free, cost-effective way to hamstring the Soviets—and, importantly, by their fellow Muslims, who came to Afghanistan by the thousands to wage jihad (holy war) against the invaders. When Afghanistan's Communist government finally collapsed in 1992, efforts to build a broadly representative government among guerrilla factions collapsed, and for several years chaos reigned. In the mid-1990s, a group of puritanical Muslim fighters known as the Taliban were able to seize control of most of the country and bring order. The peace the Taliban brought, however, was the oppressive peace of the religious fanatic. Moreover, Afghanistan under the Taliban became home to every kind of Muslim militant organization, including Osama bin Laden's al-Qaeda.

On September 19, 2001, the United States dispatched more than 100 combat and support aircraft to various bases in the Middle East and the Indian Ocean. A large naval task force was sent to join what was first called Operation Infinite Justice but later, after some Muslims indicated that the name was offensive, was renamed Operation Enduring Freedom. Japan—which along with Germany was able to overcome its post–World War II angst about deploying troops abroad—sent three warships to support the effort, although they were restricted to a noncombat role according to the terms of Japan's constitution.

Allied air strikes in Afghanistan began on October 7. Later U.S. special forces, including Delta Force and Rangers, launched ground raids inside the country. The United States enlisted as an ally an anti-Taliban group known as the Northern Alliance, which was the principal remaining opposition to the Taliban in Afghanistan, relying on them to provide the bulk of ground troops for the campaign. The northern city of Mazar-e Sharif fell a month later, and on November 13 U.S. troops and Northern Alliance fighters entered the Afghan capital, Kabul, as Taliban forces fled the city.

With the fall of the Taliban's principal city of Kandahar imminent, American B-52 bombers began bombing a network of caves in the so-called Tora Bora mountains of eastern Afghanistan, the last stronghold of forces loyal to Osama bin

Laden and to the Taliban. On December 15 anti-Taliban Afghan troops, backed by British and American commandos, surrounded a cave where they thought bin Laden and a dwindling force of al-Qaeda fighters were hiding, but he was not found. Bin Laden apparently fled the country undetected, and his whereabouts and those of Taliban leader Muhammad Omar were to remain a matter of speculation.

Ethnic and tribal rivalry were prominent in Afghanistan in the following years, yet important steps were taken toward building a stable, democratic social structure based on traditional Afghan values. Hamid Karzai, picked in December 2001 to head an interim authority in Afghanistan by a UN-sponsored international conference in Bonn, Germany, sought to maintain balance among the country's ethnic and tribal groups while laying a foundation for national institutions. Karzai had no armed group of his own, so security in Kabul was maintained by an International Security Assistance Force (ISAF) of 4,000 to 5,000 international troops whose command was rotated among various participating countries.

U.S. troops did not participate in the ISAF, but they operated throughout the country in an attempt to root out fighters loyal to the ousted Taliban regime and to eradicate remnants of al-Qaeda. U.S. military reports of a large-scale operation in March 2002 near the Pakistani border claimed that hundreds of holdouts had been killed. Most Afghans did not view U.S. forces in Afghanistan as invaders, however, and many constructive results of their intervention were welcomed. Still, as months grew into years, increasing numbers of Afghan civilian casualties from American military activity provoked criticism from some who opposed Karzai's friendly relations with the United States.

In April 2002, the country's former king, Mohammad Zahir Shah, returned to Kabul after an exile of 29 years. Many hoped that the king's return would lead to the reestablishment of Afghanistan's Pashtun monarchy, but Zahir Shah himself ruled this out. In June, however, the former king officially opened a special Loya Jirga (grand council), as prescribed by the Bonn

Agreement. An assembly of the most important leaders from across Afghanistan, the Loya Jirga embodied supreme authority in Afghanistan's political life.

The Loya Jirga's most important task was to choose a president of the transitional authority that, according to the Bonn Agreement, should replace the interim authority. Karzai was expected to be elected, and challenges from former president Burhaneddin Rabbani, a Tajik, and from supporters of the former king were avoided when both men withdrew their names from consideration in a demonstration of national unity. The Loya Jirga then approved Karzai and 13 members of his cabinet. An additional 16 ministers were named by Karzai only after the Loya Jirga had adjourned. By late June, Karzai's administration had been expanded to include four vice presidents, one each from Afghanistan's four major ethnic groups, the Pashtun, Tajik, Uzbek, and Hazara.

Still, violence persisted, with a spate of political assassinations, car bombings, and guerrilla attacks. These included attacks on high-ranking Afghan officials. In September, Karzai himself narrowly escaped the bullets of a gunman who attacked his car. These and other incidents during the year demonstrated the government's continued vulnerability to breakdowns in public security.

Afghanistan continued to work toward stabilization and reconstruction in 2003, but uneven progress and fears over security throughout the country left Karzai's precarious transitional authority vulnerable to charges of impotence and a target for groups hostile to its international supporters. Well-wishers of the administration could point to a number of positive developments, but most of them were balanced by negative or uncertain realities.

Nonetheless, following the timetable fixed by the Bonn Agreement, preparations were made to register Afghans for a general election in June 2004. In November 2003, the government announced the draft of a new constitution that was submitted to a special Loya Jirga in December. Some Afghans criticized the government for having invited public debate only after the constitution was drafted, and many, both in and out of the government, advocated strict accordance with Shari'ah (Islamic law) in the development of a new legal framework. Lack of security throughout the country continued to cause some, including UN special representative Lakhdar Brahimi, to doubt the possibility of conducting fair elections on schedule.

Despite continued security concerns, 2003 brought several developments that hinted at a return to normalcy. First, Kabul experienced something of an economic boom, with the increase of reconstruction projects paid for with international assistance. Though much of the $4.5 billion international donors had pledged previously to Afghanistan's reconstruction had not arrived or had already been consumed as humanitarian aid, in the summer the United States said it would increase its reconstruction aid by $900 million.

Second, more than 2.5 million refugees and internally displaced persons had returned voluntarily to their homes, though food shortages and an increased cost of living threatened some, especially landless returnees and households headed by women. Many refugees, even those who had been living for years in camps in neighboring Iran or Pakistan, had become accustomed to electricity and schools. When the country's school system reopened in March, 5 million students, boys and girls (girls and women had been denied education under the Taliban), enrolled. Construction on the Kabul–Kandahar–Herat highway reached Kandahar, restoring a vital part of the overland route linking Europe and the Middle East with South Asia.

Security, particularly in rural areas, continued to be a concern. Although U.S. Defense Secretary Donald Rumsfeld visited Kabul in May 2003 and declared that major combat activity by U.S. forces there was over, Operation Enduring Freedom continued to occupy more than 10,000 U.S. and coalition troops against the Taliban and al-Qaeda militants as well as against smaller militant groups from the Afghan War that had resurfaced in the post-Taliban era.

On October 9, 2004, Afghanistan held its first national election in thirty-five years. Amid charges of voting irregularities—largely discounted by international observers—Hamid Karzai won a solid majority of the vote and was sworn in as president of Afghanistan on December 7, 2004.

Ahmadinejad, Mahmoud

Mahmoud Ahmadinejad, also spelled Mahmud Ahmadinezhad, is an Iranian revolutionary and politician who became Iran's president in 2005. Born in 1956 in Garmsar, a town southeast of Tehran, Ahmadinejad's family moved to Tehran when he was a child. He was raised in poor and turbulent southern Tehran during the reign of Mohammad Reza Shah Pahlavi. Ahmadinejad graduated from secondary school in 1975 and afterward studied engineering at Iran University of Science and Technology, an institution where the future president also later obtained his doctorate (1997) in civil engineering. In 1979, during the Islamic revolution, he joined a political organization called the Office of Strengthening Unity (OSU; Persian: Daftar-e Tahkim-e Vahdat),

Mahmoud Ahmadinejad.

whose goal was to combine the efforts of students from secular schools and from seminaries in countering the influence of the quasi-Marxist organization Mojahedin-e Khalq (People's Fighters) at Iranian universities. Later that year members of the OSU overran the U.S. embassy in Tehran, taking 66 U.S. citizens hostage there and at the Iranian Foreign Ministry.

After Iraq invaded Iran in 1980, Ahmadinejad joined the Revolutionary Guard Corps, where he was apparently a senior officer in that unit's special operations brigade. At the end of the war he held several provincial administrative posts before being appointed governor-general of the newly formed province of Ardabil in 1993. He took a teaching position at his alma mater in 1997 and in 2003 was appointed mayor of Tehran by a newly elected, conservative town council. As mayor, he stressed a return to the religious principles first put forward by revolutionary leader Ruhollah Khomeini, to whose conservative values the young mayor remained devoted.

In 2005 Ahmadinejad was one of a handful of candidates on the ballot for president in an election that heavily favored former president Ali Akbar Hashemi Rafsanjani. He defeated Rafsanjani in a runoff ballot by stressing social and economic justice for Iran's working class and poor (a theretofore untapped section of the electorate) and by characterizing himself as battling against a corrupt and unresponsive system that had deserted revolutionary values.

Armed Forces

Under Mohammad Reza Shah Pahlavi, Iran had one of the largest armed forces in the world, but it quickly dissolved with the collapse of the monarchy in 1979. Reconstituted following the revolution, the Iranian military engaged in a protracted war with Iraq (the Iran-Iraq War, 1980–1990) and has since maintained formidable active and reserve components. Since the mid-1980s Iran has sought to establish programs to develop weapons of mass destruction, including nuclear, biological, and chemical weapons (Iran used the latter in its war with Iraq), and by the late 1990s it had achieved some success in the domestic production of medium- and intermediate-range missiles—effective from 300 to 600 miles and from 600 to 3,300 miles away, respectively. Outside observers, particularly those within the United States, have contended that Iran's fledgling nuclear energy industry is the seedbed for a nuclear weapons program.

Iran's military obtains much of its manpower from conscription, and males are required to serve 21 months of military service. The army is the largest branch of Iran's military, followed by the Revolutionary Guards. This body, organized in the republic's early days, is the country's most effective military force and consists of the most politically dependable and religiously devout personnel. Any security forces that are involved in external war or in armed internal conflict are either accompanied or led by elements of the Revolutionary Guards. Iran has only a small air force and navy. A national police force is responsible for law enforcement in the cities, and a gendarmerie oversees rural areas.

"Axis of Evil"

In his January 2002 State of the Union address, U.S. President George W. Bush reflected on the terrorist attacks of September 11, the subsequent invasion of Afghanistan, and the general war on terrorism, which had become the top priority of his administration and the U.S. government at every level. Most significantly, he effectively broadened the antiterrorist struggle by declaring that nations attempting to produce "weapons of mass destruction" (WMD) were part of the world terrorist threat. He specifically named Iran, Iraq, and North Korea as an "axis of evil" that was developing nuclear, chemical, or biological weaponry, and he challenged other governments to confront these states as well. The speech set the tone for a period in which the new terrorist threat dominated foreign relations as well as U.S. domestic politics.

However, dramatic developments in the war on terrorism were rare during 2002. In March, U.S. forces led a successful March coalition military effort in Afghanistan, dubbed Operation Anaconda, that killed an estimated 500 Taliban and al-Qaeda fighters, but the top al-Qaeda and Taliban leaders, Osama bin Laden and Mohammad Omar, remained at large, and rumors of bin Laden's death were never confirmed. Despite plentiful alarms, there were no new terrorist attacks on American soil. The person or persons who sent a series of anthrax-laced letters through U.S. postal facilities in late 2001, killing five Americans, were not identified, and no connection between those events and the events of September 11 was established. Nonetheless, a political consensus developed behind the main elements of the president's drive to increase domestic precautions against terrorist attacks—to beef up military preparedness and to lead the world response to the threat.

Bush proposed a 14 percent increase for defense spending, raising it to $379 billion annually, the largest increase in two decades, and he sought to double expenditures for homeland security, to $37.7 billion. Some of the president's proposals, however, became entangled in politics. Numerous U.S. allies, including top officials of otherwise stalwart European allies, faulted Bush's approach as excessively unilateral and jingoistic. Two key parts of Bush's antiterrorism legislative package— establishment of a new federal Department of Homeland Security and the provision of federal terrorism reinsurance— became stalled in the U.S. Senate owing to objections from labor unions and trial lawyers. They were belatedly approved only after the November 2002 election, along with a measure creating a bipartisan commission to study intelligence failures preceding the September 11 attacks. Most administration initiatives, however, including a major bioterrorism defense bill increasing vaccine stockpiles and protecting water and food supplies, were swiftly put into place.

Congress also accepted in 2002 Bush's expanded definition of the war on terrorism, including—in principle—his call for an end to the Ba'th regime in Iraq. In October, only days before fall elections, both chambers overwhelmingly approved a resolution authorizing the use of force to topple Saddam Hussein in Iraq.

U.S. allies overwhelmingly supported the 2001 incursion into Afghanistan, but the Bush administration's stepped up aggressiveness toward perceived terrorist threats in 2002, directed initially at Iraq, attracted numerous skeptics, especially in Europe and the Middle East, who complained about what they saw as U.S. hubris and an unwillingness by the Bush administration to consult and work with its allies. The new U.S. line was formalized in September in a document, "National Security Strategy of the United States—2002," which promised U.S. preemptive removal of WMD from those deemed to be a national enemy. "The gravest danger our nation faces lies at the crossroads of radicalism and technology. . . . In the new world we have entered, the only path to peace and security is the path of action," the Bush administration declared.

Only a handful of countries, including Britain and Australia, endorsed the preemption policy openly. Reactions in France and Germany were hostile. German Chancellor Gerhard Schröder, running for reelection in the period leading to the Iraq invasion, repeatedly promised that his administration would never join any U.S. war effort against Iraq. In September, Bush appeared before the United Nations to urge multilateral support for disarming Iraq in accordance with agreements made following the First Persian Gulf War (1990–1991). After an uncomfortable delay, the UN Security Council unanimously approved a strong resolution demanding that the Iraqi government, led by Saddam Hussein, admit UN weapons inspectors with intrusive authority. Both France and Russia made it clear, however, that their involvement in any potential military action against Iraq would require specific UN approval.

Saddam's government eventually provided a catalog of facilities, products, and scientists and submitted to an inspection regime. At the end of 2002 the U.S.-Iraqi face-off intensified as inspectors examined Iraqi sites. Meanwhile, both sides worked a clamorous public relations strategy, with U.S. authorities proclaiming that Iraqis were violating their obligations by resisting enforcement of U.S.-led no-fly zones and Iraqis insisting that inspections had found nothing incriminating. The inspectors were not scheduled to report their findings until early 2003, but by year's end a U.S.-dominated coalition had more than 100,000 troops either deployed or en route to staging areas around Iraq.

In early fall 2002, even as the United States was focusing diplomatic and military efforts on Iraq, the second "axis of evil" country, North Korea, entered again into world headlines. Confronted with evidence that its scientists had been working on a uranium-enrichment program in apparent violation of a 1994 promise to refrain from such activity, North Korean officials freely admitted the violation and implied that they were working on nuclear weapons as well. Under the 1994 pact, negotiated in part by former U.S. President Jimmy Carter, North Korea had agreed to accept two light-water reactors and 500,000 tons of heavy fuel oil annually from the United States in exchange for a freeze on its development of a nuclear program that could also produce nuclear weapons. North Korean officials followed the admission with further breaches, expelling International Atomic Energy Agency inspectors, removing surveillance cameras and seals from key sites, and restarting a nuclear plant using fuel rods that, when spent, could be used to produce weapons-grade plutonium.

Some analysts suggested that North Korean autocrat Kim Jong Il was using a renewed nuclear threat to extort additional concessions from the West. North Korea, a land of scant resources, has devoted most of them to military purposes and has depended on outside assistance to thwart famine, power shortages, and hardship for its 22 million citizens. The collapse of the Soviet Union in the early 1990s deprived the North Koreans of aid they greatly needed, and a series of bad harvests in subsequent years may have brought the North Korean economy to the point of collapse. Other analysts suggested that Kim, sensing that North Korea would be the next target of President Bush's campaign against the "axis of evil," was arming himself with a nuclear deterrent. In any event, the Bush administration refused to negotiate with the North Koreans, and U.S. Secretary of Defense Donald Rumsfeld pointedly warned that the Pentagon was prepared to fight a second war if Kim felt "emboldened" because of the American preoccupation with Iraq.

The third country cited by Bush in his "axis of evil" speech was Iran, which had continued to engage in programs to develop WMD at least since the Iran-Iraq War (1980–1990), during which both Iran and Iraq used chemical weapons on each other's troops (and Iraq used them on its own Kurdish population). In fact, a number of analysts concluded that the development of WMD in both Iran and Iraq was a response to the threat, real or imagined, of each for the other. Iran was believed to have been stockpiling chemical weapons since the 1980s, but the greater threat was often cited as its development of nuclear weapons in concert with its programs to produce medium- and intermediate-range ballistic missiles. Iran claimed that the domestically mined uranium under enrichment was needed as fuel for a series of nuclear reactors the country was planning. But it was widely believed, both in Europe and in the United States, that this refinement process may also have been intended for the creation of weapons-grade uranium. (The enrichment process for producing fuel and weapons-grade uranium is virtually the same.)

In March 2003, despite a sluggish economy and the multiple burdens of an unprecedented war on terrorism, and although France, Germany, and Russia had refused to allow a UN vote authorizing it, the United States initiated its second major military incursion in a Muslim country in 18 months when it led an invasion of Iraq. Backed by a handful of major countries, dubbed by Bush the "coalition of the willing," the United States in early spring overran Iraq in a little over three weeks. While major combat was over quickly, an untidy aftermath in Iraq seriously strained both American military resources and the national will. The aggressive U.S. action, grounded in a new assertion of the right to wage "preemptive war" against terrorists, badly divided the country's traditional allies and energized a long-dormant antiwar faction in the domestic body politic, particularly because the Iraqi weapons that had served as the major pretext for war were never found.

The war on terrorism, including the Iraq invasion, continued to dominate both U.S. domestic policy and foreign politics. The new U.S. preemptive-war policy, and particularly its action in Iraq, fractured U.S. relations with several European powers. Traditional allies of the United States, led by France and Germany, declined to commit troops to the Iraq operation, nor did they share in the costs of putting Iraq back on its feet or provide troops to maintain order. In September 2003, the Bush administration acknowledged reluctantly that reconstruction costs in Iraq and Afghanistan would require $86 billion in additional U.S. funds. After extended controversy, the U.S. Congress eventually approved the outlay.

Concerns over nuclear proliferation in developing countries have continued to preoccupy U.S. policy makers. In 2003, North Korea withdrew from the Nuclear Nonproliferation Treaty, the first signatory ever to do so, and threatened to resume its nuclear-weapons program. North Korea insisted on direct negotiations with the United States that would be preceded by a U.S. agreement not to attack it. Six-country talks, including North Korea's ally China, were held without apparent progress, but after the United States offered limited security promises, negotiations were resumed.

Iran and Libya, under international pressure, promised to open their long-running and secretive nuclear programs to inspection. Iran revealed that its efforts had been under way for 18 years, which prompted some within the United States to call for punitive measures, but UN authorities elected instead to push only for more effective future inspections. Libya, which somehow had avoided characterization within the "axis of evil," struggled to escape UN economic sanctions—and agreed to pay $2.7 billion to families of victims killed in the bombing of a U.S. airliner over Lockerbie, Scotland, in 1988. A Scottish court had convicted a Libyan intelligence agent in the attack. Later in 2003, a shipment of centrifuge equipment heading to Libya was intercepted at an Italian port, the first action under a U.S.-led 11-nation Proliferation Security Initiative. Within weeks the Libyan regime publicly disclosed its own nuclear-weapons-development program and promised to dismantle it. Supporters of the Bush administration attributed this progress on nuclear nonproliferation to the forceful approach taken by the United States in Iraq.

As part of an agreement with a delegation from European countries, Iran agreed in late 2004 to stop its enrichment of uranium, only to announce in May 2005 that it would resume production. European leaders, upset by this action, continued

to push for a negotiated settlement with Iran that would continue Iran's adherence to the Nuclear Nonproliferation Treaty
and its cooperation with the International Atomic Energy
Agency. Fears that the United States would opt for a military
solution to Iran's uranium refinement were accentuated by
the Bush administration's refusal to rule out a military strike
against Iran and by the fact that the United States occupied two
countries bordering Iran—Iraq and Afghanistan.

A Closer Look
Bush, Iraq, and the World
by Strobe Talbott

From the moment that the first explosions lit up the night sky over Baghdad, this war was personal. Four huge bombs and about 40 cruise missiles slammed into a heavily fortified VIP compound near the Tigris River. The opening salvo was intended not just to inspire "shock and awe" among the Iraqi people but to kill their leader, Saddam Hussein. "Selected targets of military importance," said President George W. Bush when he went on national television half an hour later. "A target of opportunity," added White House and Pentagon sources in the hours that followed. They left no doubt who was in the crosshairs.

Bush had come by his animus honestly. The greatest triumph of the presidency of his father, George H. W. Bush, had been to end Saddam's occupation of Kuwait in the First Persian Gulf War (1990–1991). But that victory had been incomplete. Saddam survived, and two years later he plotted to assassinate the senior Bush, who was then out of office, during a visit to Kuwait.

No wonder the second President Bush felt he had a score to settle. He also had objective reasons to wish for Saddam's demise, as did the whole world. The Iraqi dictator was an affront to the very idea of an international community. He had spent the 1990s intimidating his neighbors, brutalizing his own people, engaging in genocidal repression of Iraq's Marsh Arabs and Kurds, and systematically flouting the terms of probation that the UN had imposed on him after his eviction from Kuwait. Saddam played cat and mouse with the UN as it tried to make sure he was not illicitly developing chemical, biological, or nuclear weapons. In 1998 the UN withdrew its arms inspectors in the face of Iraqi deceit, defiance, and obstruction.

So, in addition to its being personal for President Bush, this was a war waiting to happen. Whenever it had occurred and however it was explained from the bully pulpit in Washington, it would have set off a wave of criticism and second-guessing around the world. For at least half a century, the emergence of the United States as the strongest nation in history had aroused a combination of ambivalence and resentment in other countries, including friends and allies of the United States. They counted on the strength of the American economy to boost their own, admired the United States for its political values and the dynamism of its culture and society, and looked to Washington for protection. However, when American presidents—in disregard of John Quincy Adams's famous advice—went abroad in search of monsters to destroy, the foreign reaction to success was two cheers, not three, and the reaction to failure was varying degrees of schadenfreude.

President John F. Kennedy took his lumps abroad as well as at home for botching an attempt to eliminate Fidel Castro in Cuba. Lyndon Johnson's debacle in Vietnam was widely seen as Goliath meeting his match. Ronald Reagan made quick work of tiny Grenada in 1983, but the pretext for the invasion—the rescue of American students at a beachfront medical school—struck many as implausible and unjustified. In addition to his own showdown with Saddam Hussein, George H. W. Bush went into Panama with guns blazing, kicked down the door, and dragged the country's strongman, Manuel Noriega, off to an American jail. By what right? asked many, especially in Latin America, which has had long experience with "Tío Sam" armed with a pistol and a "Wanted Dead or Alive" poster.

Under President Bill Clinton, the United States resorted to force on a significant scale three times: in 1994, when it replaced a military junta in Haiti with the democratically elected president; and in 1995 and 1999, when it conducted bombing campaigns to stop Slobodan Milosevic's rampages of ethnic cleansing in the Balkans. Once again the reaction abroad to the United States' actions was a mixture of astonishment (sometimes tinged with anxiety) at U.S. military prowess; gratitude (sometimes grudging) for American leadership; and unease at the unprecedented, unrivaled, and unregulated extent of American power. When in 1999 French Foreign Minister Hubert Védrine labeled the U.S. *l'hyperpuissance*, or "the hyperpower," he did not mean it as a compliment, and he had in mind the foreign policy of the archmultilateralist Clinton.

It was against this backdrop that George W. Bush became the custodian of all that power in January 2001. Yes, he had a glint of vengeance in his eye on the subject of Saddam, and yes, he slipped naturally into the Gary Cooper role as the marshal in *High Noon*—facing down the bad guys while the frightened townspeople disappear from the streets, duck behind closed doors, and peek out through drawn blinds. But he also had a strong case, and plenty of precedent, for making the downfall of an international outlaw a priority of his foreign policy.

However, the Second Persian Gulf War as waged by the second President Bush proved to be more controversial abroad than any other American military adventure since Vietnam—which is all the more extraordinary in that it took only six weeks and relatively little death and destruction for the United States to accomplish its immediate objectives. The war was seen as dramatic evidence of what many had feared for over two years. From virtually the day he took office, Bush had put the world on notice that the executive branch of the U.S. government was operating under a new concept of the American mission and how to accomplish it. Previously, the assumption had been: "Together if we can, alone if we must." "Together" meant a preference for working with allies, with regional security organizations, and with the authorization of UN Security Council resolutions. The Bush administration stood the formula on its head: "Alone if we can, together if we must."

In one respect this shift was unabashedly political. Spokesmen for the new administration claimed that Democrats—particularly the one who occupied the presidency between the two Bushes—had diluted the United States' power, squandered the nation's resources, and emboldened its enemies. They had done so through misplaced idealism about the nature of the world, a naive belief in the illusory if not oxymoronic concept of international law, excessive deference to the sensibilities of other countries (notably including allies), a foolish reliance on feckless international organizations, and a timidity about the decisive use of U.S. force.

While this critique was directed primarily against Clinton, it was, ironically though inescapably, also a tacit put-down of the elder Bush's concept, enunciated in 1991, that the end of the Cold War made possible a "new world order," led by the United States but based on collaboration with old friends and new partners and the strengthening of international institutions.

During the first nine months of 2001, the administration made statements and took actions intended to demonstrate a new self-reliance and assertiveness and, accordingly, a new resistance to agreements and arrangements that limited the United States' freedom of action. The United States renounced, "unsigned," weakened, disdained, or ignored more than a dozen treaties and diplomatic works in progress that it had inherited from its predecessors, Republican as well as Democratic. These included the Kyoto Protocol on climate change, the International Criminal Court, the Treaty on Anti-Ballistic Missile Systems, the land-mine-ban treaty, and an array of conventions designed to protect the rights of children, stop torture, curb discrimination by race and gender, end the production of biological weapons, prevent money laundering, and limit trafficking in small arms. Earlier administrations had had objections to some features of many of these accords but had sought to improve them; the Bush administration seemed to want nothing to do with agreements of this kind.

The new U.S. leadership also downgraded the importance it

attached to diplomacy, since that is an exercise in compromise and the Bush team was not in a compromising mood. The United States suspended the Middle East peace process and the dialogue with North Korea.

By the late summer of 2001, there was more grumbling than ever before from those around the world who were prepared to follow the U.S. president as a leader but were less inclined to take orders from him as a boss. Vice President Dick Cheney and Secretary of Defense Donald Rumsfeld quickly established themselves as the advocates, in public and in the councils of the administration, of unilateralism without apologies. Secretary of State Colin Powell seemed to be alone in voicing a more traditional, cooperative, and institutional approach. He lost one battle after another, and his imminent resignation was frequently rumored.

Then came September 11. The immediate effect of the attacks was to galvanize international sympathy for the United States. There was a sudden burst of approval for President Bush as a righteous lawman, and the world became one big posse. The normally *hyperpuissance*-bashing Paris daily *Le Monde* ran a banner headline proclaiming, "We are all Americans now."

Secretary Powell went from being the odd man out to being the man of the hour. He assembled an international coalition of unprecedented breadth to back the United States as it prepared for retribution against Afghanistan, which had become a breeding ground for radical Islamists and a sanctuary for Osama bin Laden and his al-Qaeda terrorist network.

The Bush administration was glad to have good wishes and political support from abroad. But when NATO, for the first time in its history, invoked Article 5 of its charter, proclaiming that the assaults against the World Trade Center and the Pentagon constituted an attack on all member states, the United States said, in effect, "Thanks very much; now please stay out of the way while we take care of this." As a result, the alliance was largely sidelined during the military action in Afghanistan.

Only when the Afghan Taliban had been driven from power

and the United States turned to the hard work of reconstruction did it welcome international participation. One reason was that the Bush administration saw itself as doing regime change but not nation building. Another was that it wanted, as quickly as possible, to get on with changing another regime—in Iraq. The day after September 11, Paul Wolfowitz, Rumsfeld's intellectually formidable and politically powerful deputy, made the case in a meeting with the president that once the United States had taken care of Target Kabul, it should turn to Target Baghdad.

The willingness of the American people to support military action in Iraq increased because of September 11. Before the terror attacks, the term *national security* had been an abstraction for many Americans. Afterward it had new, concrete meaning virtually synonymous with personal safety. The world was a place where bad people—"evildoers," as the president put it— were looking for ways to kill Americans on their own territory. It was easier than it would have been otherwise for the administration to convince Americans that Saddam too was an evildoer who would kill Americans if he could and that the United States therefore had to kill him first. That was the subtext of the doctrine that the administration promulgated a year after September 11 in a presidential document identifying preemptive and preventive war as vital tools for the defense of the homeland.

In a speech to the Veterans of Foreign Wars in August 2002, Vice President Cheney set the stage for applying the new doctrine to Iraq. "We must take the battle to the enemy," he said. "We" meant the United States; the United Nations, Cheney made clear, had disqualified itself and should step aside.

In a phrase that had gained currency since September 11, the administration set about "connecting the dots" between Saddam on the one hand and weapons of mass destruction (WMD) and the forces of international terrorism on the other. Since Saddam was trying to acquire WMD and might give them to terrorists, the United States should bring him down. Embedded in this syllogism was a major weakness in the administration's case for war. In his effort to build domestic and international support for military action, Bush was driven to assert—and, as it turned out, exaggerate—the extent of Saddam's WMD programs and his ties to terrorists.

The most vocal skeptics about the logic of the administration's argument were Republicans associated with the first President Bush, particularly former national security adviser Brent Scowcroft and former secretary of state James Baker. Whatever the misgivings of prominent Democrats, they were reluctant to tackle a president who was riding high largely because of his robust response to September 11. Within the administration, Powell continued to be a force for moderation. He persuaded Bush to address the UN and give multilateralism one more chance. The president dared the UN to prove itself relevant but, unlike Cheney, did not dismiss its ability to do so. The challenge led directly to the unanimous passage of Security Council Resolution 1441, which warned of "serious consequences" if Iraq did not comply with tough new inspections. Saddam immediately adopted his familiar practice of dodging and weaving, but it looked as though the United States might finally have laid the basis for a UN-authorized, U.S.-led military action.

Had it worked out that way, the Second Persian Gulf War would have been part of the continuum going back to the First Persian Gulf War and the Clinton administration's use of force in Haiti and the Balkans. Not only would Bush have prevailed over Saddam, but he would have had the much-vaunted international community largely behind him—and, indeed, with him on the ground in large and diverse numbers.

Instead, the juggernaut that Bush and Powell had put in motion turned into a train wreck, primarily between the United States and France. President Jacques Chirac shares the blame. In an interview on March 10, 2003, he warned that France would veto a new resolution authorizing force under any circumstances. Russia and China, which were prepared to go along with France in either direction, took a similar position.

Chirac's obstinacy and grandstanding cut the legs out from under Powell and strengthened those in the administration who had warned that by going to the UN in the first place, the president had fallen into a trap. Now the United States was, in the eyes of the unilateralists, free to do the job right, with a "coalition" that included, in its military dimension, Great Britain, Australia, and Poland, as well as some crucial logistic support from the smaller Persian Gulf states.

Operation Iraqi Freedom produced two positive results. First, it rid Iraq, the region, and the world of a scourge; and second, in part because of an understanding he had with British Prime Minister Tony Blair, his staunchest ally, Bush relaunched the Middle East peace process.

On the other hand, the war did profound damage to American relations with a wide array of countries and several international institutions, principally the UN and NATO, which were further marginalized. More generally, it heightened anxieties that American power, benevolent though its motivations might be, was a problem for virtually every other country on Earth, especially if the victory in Iraq vindicated the unilateralists and ensured their continued ascendancy in the United States. As American and British troops were tearing down Saddam's statues and scouring the country for the man himself, many around the world (and in the United States as well) feared that the "Iraq model" would serve as a template for changing two other regimes that Bush had named as part of the "axis of evil," Iran and North Korea, since both had nuclear-weapons programs far more advanced than Iraq's.

It was not that simple, however. In the second half of 2003, the U.S. military had its hands full in Iraq and Afghanistan, both of which were far from stabilized. Partly for that reason, and also because the United States needed as much international help as possible for the jobs ahead in those two countries, the administration put its six-shooter back in its holster and resorted to multilateral diplomacy in trying to deal with Iran and North Korea. Just as it quickly became apparent that the

Iraq war would have a long, messy, and uncertain aftermath, so the struggle to define the future of American foreign policy was far from over. What was already being called the "Bush revolution" in U.S. foreign policy might yet give way to at least a partial restoration of traditional American internationalism.

Strobe Talbott is a former journalist for Time *and deputy secretary of state (1994–2001), and is currently president of the Brookings Institution, Washington, D.C.*

Clerics

There is no concept of ordination in Islam, hence the role of clergy is not played by a priesthood but by a community of scholars (Arabic *'ulama'*). To become a member of the Shi'ite *'ulama'*, a male Muslim need only attend a traditional Islamic college, or *madrasah*. The main course of study in such an institution is Islamic jurisprudence (Arabic *fiqh*), but a student need not complete his *madrasah* studies to become a *faqih*, or jurist. In Iran such a low-level clergyman is generally referred to by the generic term mullah (Arabic *al-mawla*, "lord"; Persian *mulla*) or *akhund* or, more recently, *ruhani* (Persian "spiritual"). To become a mullah, one need merely advance to a level of scholarly competence recognized by other members of the clergy. Mullahs staff the vast majority of local religious posts in Iran.

An aspirant gains the higher status of *mujtahid*—a scholar competent to practice independent reasoning in legal judgment (Arabic *ijtihad*)—by first graduating from a recognized *madrasah* and obtaining the general recognition of his peers and then, most important, by gaining a substantial following among the Shi'ite community. A contender for this status is ordinarily referred to by the honorific *hojatoleslam* (Arabic *hujjat al-islam*, "proof of Islam"). Few clergymen are eventually recognized as *mujtahids*, and some are honored by the term ayatollah (Arabic *ayat allah*, "sign of God"). The honorific of grand ayatollah (*ayat allah al-'uzma'*) is conferred only upon those Shi'ite *mujtahids* whose level of insight and expertise in Islamic canon law has risen to the level of one who is worthy of being a *marja'-e taqlid* (Arabic *marja' al-taqlid*, "model of emulation"), the highest level of excellence in Iranian Shi'ism.

There is no real religious hierarchy or infrastructure within Shi'ism, and scholars often hold independent and varied views on political, social, and religious issues. Hence these honorifics are not awarded but attained by scholars through general consensus and popular appeal. Shi'ites of every level defer to clergymen on the basis of their reputation for learning and judicial acumen, and the trend has become strong in modern Shi'ism for every believer, in order to avoid sin, to follow the teachings of his or her chosen *marja'-e taqlid*. This has increased the power of the *'ulama'* in Iran, and it has also enhanced their role as mediators to the divine in a way not seen in Sunni Islam or in earlier Shi'ism.

The Constitutional Revolution (1905)

In 1890, the leader of Iran, Naser al-Din Shah, granted a nationwide concession over the sale and importation of tobacco products to a British citizen. However, popular protest compelled Naser al-Din to cancel the concession, demonstrating several factors of crucial significance for the years to come: first, that there existed in Iran a mercantile class of sufficient influence to make use of such broad, popular sentiment; and second, that such public outpourings of discontent could limit the scope of the shah's power. More important, the protest demonstrated the growing power of the Shi'ite clergy, members of which had played a crucial role in rallying Iranians against the monopoly and which was to have great influence over political changes to come.

The "Tobacco Riots"—as this episode came to be known—were a prelude to the Constitutional Revolution in the reign of Mozaffar al-Din Shah (1896–1907), during a time when the country suffered deep economic problems associated with its integration into a world economy. Iran had remained on the silver standard after most countries had left bimetallism for a gold standard in the late 1860s. Silver values in Iran slipped from the 1870s onward, and silver bullion drained out of the country, which lead to high rates of inflation and to bread riots. Further, in 1898 the government retained a foreign adviser to restructure the Customs Bureau. That action increased government revenue but alarmed Iranian merchants who feared further tax increases, including a substantial land tax. Merchants and landowners appealed for help to the 'ulama'—the community of Islamic scholars—with whom they had traditionally maintained close ties.

Many of the clergy had themselves become increasingly hostile to the regime because the clerics had become indignant over government interference in spheres that traditionally were administered by the clergy (such as the courts and education) and over fears that the government might tax *vaqf* land (mortmain, administered by the clergy). In a trend begun in the preceding Safavid period, a number of influential *mujtahid*s began to concern themselves with matters of government, to the point of questioning the regime's legitimacy. Even the shahs' earlier suppression of the Babi and Baha'i movements, a 19th-century Iranian sect that believed all religions are manifestations of the same god, and viewed as heresy by the majority of the Shi'ite establishment, failed to ingratiate the regime with the *'ulama'*. Together these groups—*'ulama'*, merchants, and landowners—began to criticize the privileges and protections accorded to European merchants and called for political and legal reforms.

At the same time, Iran was increasingly interacting with the West. This contact sparked an interest in democratic institutions among the members of a nascent intellectual class, which itself was a product of new, Western-style schools promoted by the shah. Encouraged by the Russian Revolution of 1905 and influenced by immigrant workers and merchants from Russian-controlled areas of Transcaucasia, the new Iranian intellectuals were, paradoxically, to find common cause with Iran's merchants and Shi'ite clergy. All aggrieved parties found an opportunity for social reform in 1905–1906, when a series of demonstrations, held in protest over the government's beating of several merchants, escalated into strikes that soon adjourned to a shrine near Tehran, which the demonstrators claimed as a *bast* (Persian "sanctuary"). While under this traditional Iranian form of sanctuary, the government was unable to arrest or otherwise molest the demonstrators, and a series of such sanctuary protests over subsequent months, combined with wide-scale general strikes of craftsmen and merchants, forced the ailing shah to grant a constitution in 1906. The first National

Consultative Assembly (the Majles) was opened in October of that year. The new constitution provided a framework for secular legislation, a new judicial code, and a free press. All these reduced the power of the royal court and religious authorities and placed more authority in the Majles, which, in turn, took a strong stand against European intervention.

Although the Majles was suppressed in 1908 under Mohammad 'Ali Shah (ruled 1907–1909) by the officers of the Persian Cossack Brigade—the shah's bodyguard and the most effective military force in the country at the time—democracy was revived the following year under the second Majles, and Mohammad 'Ali fled to Russia. Constitutionalists also executed the country's highest-ranking cleric, Sheikh Fazlullah Nuri, who had been found guilty by a reformist tribunal of plotting to overthrow the new order—an indication that not all of Iran's religious elite were proponents of reform. In addition, as part of the secular reforms introduced by the Majles, a variety of secular schools were established during that time, including some for girls, causing significant tension between sections of the clergy that had previously advocated reform and their erstwhile intellectual allies.

The end of the Majles, however, did not come as a result of internal strife. In an attempt to come to grips with Iran's ongoing financial problems, the Majles in 1911 hired another foreign financial adviser, this time an American, William Morgan Shuster, who advocated bold moves to collect revenue throughout the country. This action angered both the Russians and the British, who claimed limited sovereignty in the respective spheres of influence the two powers had carved out of Iran in 1907 (the Russians in northern Iran and the Caucasus and the British along the Persian Gulf). The Russians issued an ultimatum demanding Shuster's dismissal. When the Majles refused, Russian troops advanced toward Tehran, and the regent of the young Ahmad Shah (reigned 1909–1925) hastily dismissed Shuster and dissolved the Majles in December 1911.

Culture

Few countries enjoy a cultural heritage that is as long as Iran's, and few people are as aware of and articulate about their deep cultural traditions as Iranians are. Iran, or Persia, as a historical entity, dates to the time of the Achaemenids (about 2,500 years ago), and despite political, religious, and historic changes, Iranians maintain a deep connection to their past. Although daily life in modern Iran is closely interwoven with Shi'ite Islam, the country's art, literature, and architecture are ever-present reminders of its deep national tradition and of a broader literary culture that during the premodern period spread throughout the Middle East and South Asia. Much of Iran's modern history can be attributed to the essential tension that existed between the Shi'ite piety promoted by Iran's clergy and the Persian cultural legacy—in which religion played a subordinate role—proffered by the Pahlavi monarchy.

Despite the predominance of Persian culture, Iran remains a multiethnic state, and the country's Armenian, Azerbaijanian, Kurdish, and smaller ethnic minorities each have their own literary and historical traditions dating back many centuries, even—in the case of the Armenians—to the pre-Christian era. These groups frequently maintain close connections with the larger cultural life of their kindred outside Iran.

The important holiday of 'Ashura' commemorates the death (680) of al-Husayn ibn 'Ali, the third Shi'ite imam, at Karbala', Iraq. The theme of martyrdom, which is derived from this and other events in Shi'ite history, is a major component of modern Iranian culture. Other holidays include Nawruz, the Persian New Year, and the birthday of the 12th imam.

Persian cuisine, although strongly influenced by the culinary traditions of the Arab world and the subcontinent, is largely a product of the geography and domestic food products of Iran. Rice is a dietary staple, and meat—mostly lamb—plays a part in virtually every meal. Vegetables are central to the Iranian diet, with onions an ingredient of virtually every dish. Herding has long been a traditional part of the economy, and dairy products—milk, cheese, and particularly yogurt— are common ingredients in Persian dishes. Traditional Persian cuisine tends to favor subtle flavors and relatively simple preparations such as *khuresh* (stew) and kabobs. Saffron is the most distinctive spice used, but many other flavorings— including lime, mint, turmeric, and rosewater—are common, as are pomegranates and walnuts.

Carpet looms dot the country. Each locality prides itself on a special design and quality of carpet that bears its name, such as Kashan, Kerman, Khorasan, Esfahan, Shiraz, Tabriz, and Qom. Carpets are used locally and are exported. The handwoven-cloth industry has survived stiff competition from modern textile mills.

Iranian culture is perhaps best known for its literature, a tradition that forms an unbroken chain from early times. The great masters of the Persian language—Ferdowsi, Nezami, Hafez, Jami, and Rumi—continue to inspire Iranian authors in modern times, although publication and distribution of many classical works—deemed licentious by conservative clerics— have been difficult.

For centuries Islamic injunctions inhibited the development of formal musical disciplines, but folk songs and ancient Persian classical music were preserved through oral transmission from generation to generation. It was not until the 20th century that a music conservatory was founded in Tehran and that Western techniques were used to record traditional melodies and encourage new compositions. This trend was reversed, however, in 1979, when the former restrictions on the study and practice of music were restored. Although officially forbidden—even after the liberal reforms of the late 1990s—Western pop music is fashionable among Iranian youth, and there is a thriving trade in musical cassette tapes and compact discs. Iranian pop groups also occasionally perform, though often under threat of punishment. In 2000, Googoosh, the most popular Iranian singer of the prerevolutionary era, resumed her career—albeit from abroad—after 21 years of forced silence.

The most popular form of entertainment in Iran is the cinema, which is also an important medium for social and political commentary in a society that has had little tolerance for participatory democracy. After the 1979 revolution the government at first banned filmmaking but then gave directors financial support if they agreed to propagate Islamic values. However, the public showed little interest, and this period of ideology-driven filmmaking did not last. Soon films that dealt with the Iran-Iraq War (1980–1990) or that reflected more tolerant expressions of Islamic values, including Sufi mysticism, gained ground. The religious establishment, however, generally frowns upon the imitation of Western films among Iran's filmmakers but encourages adapting Western and Eastern classic stories and folktales, provided that they reflect contemporary Iranian concerns and not transgress Islamic restrictions imposed by the government. In the 1990s the fervor of the early revolutionary years was replaced by demands for political moderation and better relations with the West. Iran's film industry became one of the finest in the world, with festivals of Iranian films being held annually throughout the world.

Wrestling, horse racing, and ritualistic bodybuilding are the traditional sports of the country. Team sports were introduced from the West in the 20th century, the most popular being rugby football and volleyball. Under the monarchy, modern sports were incorporated into the school curricula. Iran's Physical Education Organization was formed in 1934. Iranian athletes first participated in the Olympics Games in 1948. The country made its Winter Games debut in 1956. All of Iran's Olympic medals have come in weight-lifting and wrestling events.

Football (soccer) has become the most popular game in Iran—the country's team won the Asian championships in 1968, 1974, and 1976 and made its World Cup debut in 1978—but the 1979 revolution was a major setback for Iranian sports. The new government regarded the sports stadium as a rival to the mosque. Major teams were nationalized, and women were prevented from participating in many activities. In addition, the Iran-Iraq War left few resources to devote to sports. However, the enormous public support for sports, especially for football, could not be easily suppressed. Since the 1990s there has been a revival of athletics in Iran, including women's activities. Sports have become inextricably bound up with demands for political liberalization, and nearly every major event has become an occasion for massive public celebrations by young men and women expressing their desire for reform and more amicable relations with the West.

Daily newspapers and periodicals are published primarily in Tehran and must be licensed under the press law of 1979. The publication of any anti-Muslim sentiment is strictly forbidden. Iran's Ministry of Culture and Islamic Guidance operates the Islamic Republic News Agency (IRNA). Foreign correspondents are allowed into the country on special occasions. Despite constitutional guarantees of freedom of the press, censorship by conservative elements within the government is widespread, particularly in the electronic media. Regardless, print media—newspapers, magazines, and journals—contributed greatly to the growth of political reform in Iran during the late 1990s. The most widely circulated newspapers include *Ettela'at* and *Kayhan*.

Radio and television broadcasting stations in Iran are operated by the government and reach the entire country, and some radio broadcasts have international reception. The government made possession of satellite reception equipment illegal in 1995, but the ban has been irregularly enforced, and many Iranians have continued to receive television broadcasts—including Persian-language programs—from abroad. Programs are broadcast in Persian and some foreign languages, as well as in local languages and dialects. Though basic literacy increased substantially in the years following the revolution, audiovisual media have remained much more effective than print material for disseminating information, especially in rural areas.

Cyrus the Great

Cyrus II, also known as Cyrus the Great, was the Persian conqueror who in 550 BC founded the Achaemenian dynasty, which ruled over the first Persian empire. The grandson of Cyrus I (who flourished in the late seventh century BC), he came to power by overthrowing his maternal grandfather, Astyages, the king of the Medes and overlord of the Persians. The empire Cyrus developed was thenceforth centered on Persia and included Media (roughly, northwestern Iran and modern Azerbaijan), Mesopotamia, Syria, Palestine, and much of Anatolia, including Lydia and Greek Ionia. Many of these regions fell to the Persian armies, but Cyrus conquered by diplomacy as well as by force.

The subject of a rich legend in Persia and Greece (recorded by the historian Xenophon and others), Cyrus was called the father of his people. He was also known for his tolerance and for the liberal way he treated subject peoples. Regional differences in language, culture, and religion were respected, and Cyrus was a patron of local customs, even engaging in sacrifices to local deities. He appears in the Bible as the liberator of the Jews held captive in Babylon. He died while fighting in Central Asia.

His legacy is the founding not only of an empire but also of a culture and civilization that continued to expand after his death and lasted for centuries. He exerted a strong influence on the Greeks and on the imagination of the Macedonian conqueror Alexander the Great, who later put an end to the dynasty Cyrus founded. Awarded heroic qualities in legend, Cyrus often was later revered by Persians as a figure of near-religious proportions. In 1971 Iran's Pahlavi monarchy, in an attempt to draw on this cultural heritage, celebrated the 2,500th anniversary of his founding of Cyrus's dynasty.

Darius I

Darius I, also known as Darius the Great, was one of the foremost kings of the Achaemenian dynasty. He reigned from 522 to 486 BC over an empire that ranged from the Aegean Sea to the Indus River.

Darius was born during the reign of the great conqueror Cyrus II. Darius's father was Hystaspes, a satrap (governor of a province) under Cyrus who was also a distant relative of the monarch, and Darius grew up at the royal court. After Cyrus's death, his son Cambyses II became ruler. In 522 Cambyses was overthrown—either by his brother Bardiya or by an imposter pretending to be Bardiya—and died soon after. With the help of a group of Persian nobles, Darius killed the usurper and established himself as king.

Darius spent six years putting down the revolts that stemmed from his sudden rise to power. To maintain control, he devised a strong system of government. He fixed tax rates, set up a standard coinage, and wrote a code of laws. To encourage trade, Darius repaired and completed a canal begun by the Egyptians connecting the Nile River and the Red Sea. He built roads and set up post houses to aid travelers. Under him, slaves completed building the magnificent palaces at Susa and Persepolis. To extend the empire, Darius's generals conquered Thrace and Macedonia to the west and the Punjab and much of the Indus Valley to the east. Libya became a satrapy in 512 BC.

In about 517 BC, Darius made an alliance with the Greek city-state of Athens, but in about 500 the Ionian Greeks began an uprising against Persian rule. In 490 his army was badly defeated by the Athenians at the Battle of Marathon.

Four years later, while preparing a campaign against an Egyptian rebellion, he became ill and died. His tomb was built into a cliff near Persepolis. He left a record of his reign chiseled on the side of a rocky cliff overlooking the Iranian village of Behistun.

Dynastic History

Achaemenian Dynasty

The first Persian empire was ruled by the Achaemenian dynasty from 559 to 330 BC. Cyrus II (reigned 559–c. 529 BC), who actually established the empire and from whose reign it is dated, was probably its greatest leader. Another strong leader was Darius I (522–486), who excelled as an administrator and secured the borders from external threats. Xerxes I (486–465), though lacking the administrative genius of his predecessors, was a great builder. He completed many of the buildings begun by Darius. During the time of Darius I and Xerxes I, the empire extended as far west as Macedonia and Libya and as far east as the Hyphasis (Beas) River; it stretched to the Caucasus Mountains and the Aral Sea in the north and to the Persian Gulf and the Arabian Desert in the south. These two kings each attempted to invade Greece, prompting the Greco-Persian wars. The dynasty collapsed before the invasion of Macedonian conqueror Alexander the Great.

The Achaemenian rule of conquered peoples was generally liberal, and subject people were allowed latitude to follow their religious and cultural practices; the empire itself was divided into provinces (satrapies), each administered by a satrap who underwent frequent inspections by officials reporting directly to the king.

Royal inscriptions were usually trilingual, in Old Persian, Elamite, and Akkadian; however, Aramaic, a commercial lingua franca from as far back as Babylonian times, was employed for imperial administration and diplomatic correspondence.

Building activity was extensive during the height of the

empire, and of the several Achaemenian capitals, the ruins at Pasargadae and Persepolis (both currently listed as UNESCO World Heritage sites) are probably the most outstanding. Achaemenian sculptured reliefs and a great number of smaller art objects present a remarkably unified style for the period.

Arsacid Dynasty

The Arsacid dynasty was the ruling dynasty of the Parthian empire of Persia from 247 BC to AD 224. The progenitors of the dynasty were members of the Parni tribe living east of the Caspian Sea. They entered Parthia (northeastern Iran) shortly after the death of the Macedonian conqueror Alexander the Great (323 BC) and gradually gained control over much of Iran and Mesopotamia. The dynasty claimed descent from the Achaemenian king Artaxerxes II, but this was probably a spurious attempt to gain legitimacy. The first Arsacid to gain power in Parthia was Arsaces (reigned c. 250–c. 211 BC), but the Iranian plateau was not conquered in its entirety until the time of Mithradates I (reigned 171–138 BC). Two of the dynasty's most powerful rulers were Mithradates II (reigned 123–88 BC) and Phraates III (reigned 70–58/57 BC). The empire's organization was based on practices of the Hellenistic Seleucid kingdom, and the Arsacids encouraged the development of Hellenistic cities. Their wealth was largely gained through their control of east-west trade routes, and the dynasty often found itself in conflict with the Roman Empire along its western border. In AD 224, the Sasanians, an Iranian dynasty founded by Ardashir I, overthrew them. Under the Arsacids ancient Greek was commonly used, but Parthian, a dialect of Persian, became the language of state.

Sasanian Dynasty

The Sasanian dynasty ruled ancient Iran from AD 224 to 651, after which it was eradicated by invading Arab armies. Under the leadership of the dynasty's founder, Ardashir I (reigned AD 224–241), the Sasanians overthrew the Parthians and created an empire that was constantly changing in size as it reacted to Roman and Byzantine empires to the west and to the Kushans and Hephthalites to the east. At the time of Shapur I (reigned AD 241–272), the empire stretched from the Central Asian state of Sogdiana and Iberia (Georgia), in the north, to the Mazun region of Arabia, in the south; in the east it extended to the Indus River and in the west to the upper Tigris and Euphrates river valleys.

After the end of the Hellenized Arsacid Parthian Empire, a revival of Iranian cultural particularism took place under Sasanian rule. Zoroastrianism became the state religion, and at various times followers of other faiths suffered official persecution. The government was centralized, with provincial officials directly responsible to the throne, and roads, city building, and even agriculture were financed by the government. The Pahlavi (Middle Persian) language became the parlance of state.

Under the Sasanians Iranian art experienced a general renaissance. Architecture often took grandiose proportions, such as the palaces at Ctesiphon, Firuzabad, and Sarvestan. Perhaps the most characteristic and striking relics of Sasanian art are rock sculptures carved on abrupt limestone cliffs.

During the late sixth and early seventh centuries, the Sasanians engaged in a long series of brutal wars with the Byzantine Empire that left both countries fiscally and militarily drained and ripe for conquest by Arab invaders.

"Iranian Intermezzo"

The Arab conquest of the Sasanian dynasty began in earnest in 636, with the Battle of Qadisiyyah. The Arabs soon overran the empire, and the last Sasanian king, Yazdegerd III, died a fugitive in 651. Thus began a period of Persian submergence to Arab cultural domination that lasted until the beginning of the 11th century. During this time Persian culture adopted and absorbed many elements of Arab-Islamic civilization. Most Persians became Muslims (mostly of the Sunni branch), and when Persian again became a written language, it had absorbed large elements of the Arabic language, including a large lexicon of Arabic terms. With the decline of the Muslim caliphate at the end of the 10th century, a number of small native-Persian dynasties began to appear, the first of these being the Samanid and Saffarid, but an overall Persian cultural hegemony did not appear for some centuries. After the reemergence of Persian culture in the early 11th century, various Persian, Turkic, and Mongol dynasties dominated what is now Iran. This continued until the early 15th century, when a native Persian group, the Safavid dynasty, came to dominate the region.

Safavid Dynasty

The Safavid dynasty (1501–1736) led the establishment of Shi'ite Islam as the state religion of Iran. The Safavids were originally a Sufi order, the Safawiyyah, which exchanged its Sunni affiliation for Shi'ism in 1399. The founder of the dynasty, Isma'il, as head of the Sufis of Ardabil, won enough support from the local Turkmen and other disaffected heterodox tribes to enable him to capture the city of Tabriz from the Ak Koyunlu, an Uzbek Turkmen confederation, and in July 1501 Isma'il was enthroned as shah of Azerbaijan and, soon after, of Iran. Over the next 10 years he subjugated the greater part of Iran and annexed the Iraqi provinces of Baghdad and Mosul; despite the predominantly Sunni character of this territory, he proclaimed Shi'ism the state religion.

In August 1514, Isma'il was seriously defeated by his Sunni rival, the Ottoman sultan Selim I, at the Battle of Chaldiran. Thereafter, the continuing struggle against the Sunnis—the Ottomans in the west and the Uzbeks in the northeast—cost the Safavids Kurdistan, Diyarbakir, and Baghdad; the Safavid capital had to be relocated to Esfahan.

Iran weakened appreciably during the reign of Isma'il's

eldest son, Shah Tahmasp I (1524–1576), and persistent and unopposed Turkmen forays into the country increased. In 1588 'Abbas I took the throne. Realizing the limits of his military strength, 'Abbas made peace with the Ottomans in 1590 and directed his efforts against the Uzbeks. Meeting with little success and hoping to be free of reliance on tribal levies (the Kizilbash), 'Abbas engaged (1599) the Englishman Sir Robert Sherley to direct a major army reform. Three bodies of troops were formed, all trained and armed in the European manner and paid directly from the royal treasury: the *ghulam*s (slaves), the *tofangchi*s (musketeers), and the *topchi*s (artillerymen).

With his new army, 'Abbas defeated the Ottomans in 1603, forcing them to relinquish all the territory they had seized, and captured Baghdad. He also expelled (1602, 1622) the Portuguese traders who had seized the island of Hormuz in the Persian Gulf early in the 16th century.

'Abbas's remarkable reign, with its striking military successes and efficient administrative system, raised Iran to the status of a great power. Trade with the West and industry expanded; communications improved; and the capital, Esfahan, became the center of Safavid architectural achievement. Despite the Safavid Shi'ite zeal, Christians were tolerated.

After the death of Shah 'Abbas I (1629) the Safavid dynasty lasted for about a century, but it was generally a period of decline. In 1722 Ghilzai Afghans seized Esfahan. Although Shah Tahmasp II soon recovered the capital, he only briefly held the throne; a lieutenant, Nadr Qoli Beg (the future Nadir Shah), deposed him in 1732, paving the way for a period of chaos before the coming of the Qajar dynasty in 1794.

Qajar Dynasty

The Qajar dynasty dominated Iran from 1794 until the dynasty's eclipse by the Pahlavi dynasty in 1925. In 1779, following the death of Mohammad Karim Khan Zand, the Zand dynasty ruler of southern Iran, Agha Mohammad Khan (reigned 1779–1797), a leader of the Turkmen Qajar tribe, set out to reunify Iran. By 1794 he had eliminated all his rivals, including Lotf 'Ali Khan, the last of the Zand dynasty, and had reasserted Iranian sovereignty over the former Iranian territories in Georgia and the Caucasus. In 1796 he was formally crowned as shah, or emperor. Agha Mohammad was assassinated in 1797 and was succeeded by his nephew, Fath 'Ali Shah (reigned 1797–1834). Fath 'Ali attempted to maintain Iran's sovereignty over its new territories, but he was disastrously defeated by Russia in two wars (1804–1813, 1826–1828) and thus lost Georgia, Armenia, and northern Azerbaijan. Fath 'Ali's reign saw increased diplomatic contacts with the West and the beginning of intense European diplomatic rivalries over Iran. His grandson Mohammad, who fell under the influence of Russia and made two unsuccessful attempts to capture Herat, succeeded him in 1834. When Mohammad Shah died in 1848 the succession passed to his son Naser al-Din (reigned 1848–1896), who proved, in some ways, to be the ablest and most successful of the Qajar sovereigns. During his reign Western science, technology, and educational methods were introduced into Iran and the country's modernization was begun. Naser al-Din managed the country's finances in a careless fashion, however, and his granting of concessions to foreign investors angered many in Iran.

When Naser was assassinated in 1896, the crown passed to his son Mozaffar al-Din Shah (reigned 1896–1907), a weak and incompetent ruler who was forced in 1906 to grant a constitution that called for some curtailment of monarchial power. His son Mohammad 'Ali Shah (reigned 1907–1909), with the aid of Russia, attempted to rescind the constitution and abolish parliamentary government. In so doing he aroused such opposition that he was deposed in 1909, the throne being taken by his 11-year-old son Ahmad Shah (reigned 1909–1925). The young shah proved to be pleasure-loving, effete, and incompetent and was unable to preserve the integrity of Iran or the fate of his dynasty. The occupation of Iran during World War I

(1914–1918) by Russian, British, and Ottoman troops was a blow from which Ahmad Shah never effectively recovered. A coup in 1921 led to Reza Khan (ruled as Reza Shah Pahlavi, 1925–1941), an army officer, becoming the preeminent political personality in Iran. The Majles (parliament) formally deposed Ahmad Shah in 1925, ending the Qajar dynasty.

Ebadi, Shirin

Born in 1947 in Hamada, Iran, Shirin Ebadi is an Iranian lawyer, writer, and teacher who received the Nobel Prize for Peace in 2003 for her efforts to promote democracy and human rights, especially those of women and children in Iran. She was the first Muslim woman and the first Iranian to receive the award.

Ebadi earned a law degree from the University of Tehran in 1969. She was one of the first women judges in Iran and from 1975 to 1979 was head of the city court of Tehran. After the 1979 revolution and the establishment of an Islamic republic, however, women were deemed unsuitable to serve as judges, and she was forced to resign. She then practiced law and taught at the University of Tehran, and she became an advocate for civil rights. In court Ebadi defended women and dissidents and represented many people who had run afoul of the Iranian government. She also distributed evidence implicating government officials in the murders of students at the University of Tehran in 1999, for which she was jailed for three weeks in 2000. Found guilty of "disturbing public opinion," she was given a prison term, barred from practicing law for five years, and fined, although her sentence was later suspended.

Ebadi's writings include *The Rights of the Child: A Study of Legal Aspects of Children's Rights in Iran* (1994) and *History and Documentation of Human Rights in Iran* (2000). She also was founder and head of the Association for Support of Children's Rights in Iran.

Economy

The most formidable hurdle facing Iran's economy remains its continuing isolation from the international community. This isolation has hampered the short- and long-term growth of its markets, restricted the country's access to high technology, and impeded foreign investment. Iran's isolation is a product both of the xenophobia of its more conservative politicians—who fear postimperial entanglements—and sanctions imposed by the international community, particularly the United States, which accuses Iran of supporting international terrorism.

The Iran and Libya Sanctions Act of 1996 expanded an existing U.S. embargo on the import of Iranian petroleum products to encompass extensive bans on investment by both U.S. and non-U.S. companies in Iran. These prohibitions included bans on foreign speculation in Iranian petroleum development, the export of high technology to Iran, and the import of a wide variety of Iranian products into the United States. Overtures by reform-minded Iranian politicians to open their country to foreign investment have met with limited success, but in the early 21st century U.S. sanctions remained in place.

Iran's long-term objectives since the 1979 revolution have been economic independence, full employment, and a comfortable standard of living for its citizens, but at the end of the 20th century the country's economic future was lined with obstacles. Iran's population more than doubled in that period, and its population grew increasingly young. In a country that has traditionally been both rural and agrarian, agricultural production has fallen consistently since the 1960s (by the late 1990s Iran was a major food importer), and economic hardship in the countryside has driven vast numbers of people to migrate to the largest cities. The rates of both literacy and life expectancy in Iran are high for the region, but so, too, is the unemployment rate, and inflation is regularly in the range of 20 percent annually. Iran remains highly dependent on its one major industry, the extraction of petroleum and natural gas for export, and the government faces increasing difficulty in providing opportunities for a younger, better-educated workforce, which has led to a growing sense of frustration among lower- and middle-class Iranians.

Still, the government has tried to develop the country's communication, transportation, manufacturing, and energy infrastructures (including its prospective nuclear power facilities) and has begun the process of integrating its communication and transportation systems with those of neighboring states.

The national constitution establishes specific guidelines for the administration of the nation's economic and financial resources, and after the revolution the government declared null and void any law, or section of a law, that violated Islamic principles. This prohibition restricts individuals or institutions from charging interest on loans, an action considered illegal under Islamic law, and also places limits on certain types of financial speculation. These restrictions have heretofore made Iran's participation in the international economic community problematic, which has led to harsh financial conditions and a strong reliance on local markets.

From the first years of the revolution, two different factions have sought to impose their own interpretation of Islamic economics on the government. Islamic leftists have called for extensive nationalization and expansion of a welfare state. Conservatives within the religious establishment, who have maintained strong ties to the merchant community, have defended the rights of property owners and insisted on maintaining privatization. Both factions, however, have generally supported the government's restriction on Western banking practices. Although Iran's first postrevolutionary leader, Ayatollah Ruhollah Khomeini, refused to takes sides in the leftist-conservative debate, the effects of the Iran-Iraq War (1980–1990) prompted increased state intervention in the economy. The government gained a virtual monopoly over income-producing activities by nationalizing private banks and insurance companies and increasing state control of foreign trade.

The economy continued to lag despite Iran's move away from public control of the financial system after the end of the war in 1990. The election of Mohammad Khatami as president in 1997 promised social and economic reform, and a number of key government positions were filled by reformist clergy and technocrats. Nonetheless, no steps have been taken on numerous proposed plans to reduce state control of the economy and encourage privatization, and the government's economic policies have remained unclear. U.S. sanctions have also continued to hamstring Iran's economy by restricting access to Western technology, despite the willingness of some European and East Asian companies to ignore these measures. Conservatives within Iran's government have been willing, in limited instances, to ease the restriction on interest-bearing transactions but have continued to block reformists' plans to introduce large amounts of foreign capital into the country, particularly investments from the United States. Foreign investment has remained a contentious issue because of the adverse social and political effects of foreign economic entanglements during Iran's colonial past.

In addition to the extraction of petroleum and natural gas, major economic activities include agriculture, manufacturing (including mining), and trade. Agriculture contributes about one-eighth of gross domestic product (GDP), manufacturing and mining contributes about one-fifth of GDP, and trade contributes an additional one-eighth. Major crops are wheat, sugar beets, sugarcane, potatoes, rice, and barley, as well as a wide variety of fruits and vegetables. Manufactures include handmade items such as carpets and rugs, in addition to chemicals, food products, and finished goods such as automobiles. Iran has a small military-industrial complex that produces armored vehicles and missiles. Major trading partners include Germany, Switzerland, Japan, China, and France.

Farsi and Other Languages

Slightly more than half the population speak a dialect of Persian, the predominant and official language of Iran, though a number of languages and dialects are spoken. Modern Persian is called Farsi by native speakers. Written in Arabic characters, modern Persian also has many Arabic loanwords and an extensive literature. Literary Persian, the language's more refined variant, is understood to some degree by most Iranians. Persian is also the predominant language of literature, journalism, and the sciences.

Less than one-tenth of the population speaks Kurdish, and the Lurs and the Bakhtyari both speak Luri, a language distinct from, but closely related to, Persian. Only the Armenian minority speaks Armenian, a single language of the Indo-European family. The Altaic family is represented overwhelmingly by the Turkic languages, which are spoken by roughly one-fourth of the population; most speak Azerbaijanian, a language similar to modern Turkish. The Turkmen language, another Turkic language, is spoken in Iran by only a small number of Turkmen.

Only a small percentage of the population speaks Arabic as a native tongue. The main importance of the Arabic language in Iran is historical and religious. Following the Islamic conquest of Persia, Arabic virtually subsumed Persian as a literary tongue. Since that time Persian has adopted a large number of Arabic words—perhaps one-third or more of its lexicon—and borrowed grammatical constructions from Classical and, in some instances, colloquial, Arabic.

Under the monarchy, efforts were made to purge Arabic elements from the Persian language, but these met with little success and ceased outright following the revolution. Since that time, the study of Classical Arabic, the language of the Qur'an, has been emphasized in schools, and Arabic remains the predominant language of learned religious discourse.

Before 1979, English and French, and to a lesser degree German and Russian, were widely used by the educated class. European languages are used less commonly but are still taught at schools and universities.

Flag

The Iranian national flag (pictured on the back cover) has green, white, and red horizontal stripes and a red design (a stylized coat of arms) in the center, with Arabic inscriptions along the edges of the stripes. Iran's Lion and Sun emblem was displayed on a flag as early as the 15th century, and in the late 19th century the colors green and red were added as a border to a white flag bearing those symbols. After the granting of the constitution of 1906, a tricolor typical of the national flags of many other countries was officially recognized for Iran. Its horizontal stripes of green-white-red were associated, respectively, with the Islamic faith of the country, peace, and valor. Emblazoned in the center of the white stripe was the Lion and Sun; additional symbols (the imperial crown and a wreath) were added for special purposes such as the naval ensign. Over subsequent decades, many artistic variations were made to these symbols.

In 1979 the religious movement led by Ayatollah Ruhollah Khomeini overthrew the shah and his government and altered the national flag. Although the green-white-red stripes were retained, along the bottom of the green stripe and the top of the red stripe a stylized Arabic inscription—*allahu akbar* ("God is great")—was repeated 22 times in honor of the fact that the revolution had taken place on 22 Bahram in the Iranian calendar. The words *allahu akbar* are used by the muezzin to call faithful Muslims to prayer five times a day. They are also an Islamic battle cry. In the center of the flag the Lion and Sun emblem was replaced by the new coat of arms of Iran. This stylized design has a complex set of symbolisms; it can be read as a rendition in Arabic of the word *allah* as a representation of the globe, or as two crescents. The inscriptions and central emblem are appropriate for the Iranian flag in light of the religious basis of the country's 1979 revolution and the sectarian regime subsequently established.

Iran-Contra Affair

The Iran-Contra Affair was a U.S. political scandal in which members of the U.S. National Security Council (NSC), in an effort to gain political leverage with terrorist groups in Lebanon, became involved in secret weapons transactions with Iran. In turn, some of the funds from these weapons sales were used to fund an anti-Communist insurgency group (the Contras) in Nicaragua. These and other activities either were prohibited by the U.S. Congress or violated the stated public policy of the government.

The roots of the scandal go back to the Israeli invasion of Lebanon in 1982. The original plan of the Israeli operation was to expel fighters of the Palestine Liberation Organization (PLO) from bases along the Israeli border. In fact, Israeli forces advanced far into Lebanon, eventually besieging the Lebanese capital, Beirut, a city that was already the scene of a bloody civil war in which the PLO was deeply entrenched. To avoid further bloodshed, the United States negotiated an agreement that would allow PLO fighters to evacuate Beirut and sent a detachment of Marines to help the process. In October 1983 terrorists, probably affiliated with Hezbollah (a Shi'ite group with close ties to Iran), bombed the U.S. embassy in Beirut and later blew up the U.S. Marine barracks there, killing 241 Americans. The barracks attack was then the most devastating terrorist assault ever directed against the United States. At the same time, Hezbollah began a campaign of kidnapping U.S. citizens living in Lebanon in an effort to generate political capital.

During this same period, the Reagan administration faced a crisis in El Salvador, as the country had succumbed to violence among leftist insurgents, authoritarian landowners supporting right-wing death squads, and a struggling reformist government. The sources of the insurgency appeared to be Communist Cuba and the ruling Sandinista government in Nicaragua, which had recently socialized the economy, suppressed freedom of the press and religion, and established close ties to Cuba and other Soviet bloc countries. Americans, however, became increasingly confused by evidence of atrocities on all sides and were again torn between their desire to promote human rights and their determination to halt the spread of communism. Opponents of U.S. involvement warned of another Vietnam in Central America, while supporters warned of the loss of another Latin American country to communism, as occurred with Cuba a generation earlier.

Nicaragua, meanwhile, built up—in proportion to population—one of the largest armies in the world, expanded its port facilities, and received heavy shipments of arms from the Soviet Union. The U.S. Central Intelligence Agency (CIA) used this military buildup to justify the secret mining of Nicaraguan harbors in February 1984, which, when revealed, was condemned universally. The CIA also secretly organized and supplied a force of some 15,000 anti-Sandinista fighters, known as Contras, across the border in Honduras and Costa Rica, while U.S. armed forces conducted joint maneuvers with those states along the Nicaraguan border. The ostensible purpose of such exercises was to interdict the suspected flow of arms from Nicaragua to the Salvadoran rebels. In fact, American policy aimed at provoking a popular revolt in hopes of overthrowing the Sandinistas altogether.

The U.S. public was split almost evenly on the question of support for the Nicaraguan Contras. While the Reagan Doctrine of supporting indigenous rebels, such as Savimbi's UNITA in Angola or the mujahideen in Afghanistan, appeared to be a low-risk means of countering Soviet influence, many Americans remained nervous about the possibility of deeper U.S. involvement. Congress reflected this public ambivalence by first approving funds for the Contras, then restricting the ability of federal agencies to raise or spend funds for the Contras, then reversing itself again.

In early November 1985, at the suggestion of Robert C. McFarlane, the head of the NSC, President Ronald Reagan authorized a secret initiative to sell antitank and antiaircraft missiles to Iran—then struggling in the Iran-Iraq War and hungry for weapons and spare parts—in exchange for that country's help in securing the release of Americans held hostage by groups such as Hezbollah in Lebanon.

The initiative directly contradicted the administration's publicly stated policy of refusing to negotiate with terrorists or to aid countries—such as Iran—that supported international terrorism. News of the arms-for-hostages deal, first made public in November 1986, proved intensely embarrassing to the president.

Even more damaging, however, was the announcement later that month by Attorney General Edwin Meese that a portion of the $48 million earned from the sales had been diverted to a secret fund to purchase weapons and supplies for the Contras in Nicaragua. The diversion was undertaken by an obscure NSC aide, U.S. Marine Corps Lieutenant Colonel Oliver North, with the approval of McFarlane's successor at the NSC, Rear Admiral John Poindexter. (North, as it was later revealed, had also engaged in private fund-raising for the Contras.) These activities constituted a violation of a law passed by Congress in 1984 (the second Boland Amendment) that forbade direct or indirect American military aid to the Contra insurgency.

In response to the crisis, by this time known as the Iran-Contra Affair, Reagan fired both North and Poindexter and appointed a special commission, headed by former Senator John Tower of Texas (the Tower Commission), to investigate the matter. An independent counsel, Judge Lawrence Walsh, was also appointed, and the House of Representatives and the Senate began joint hearings to examine both the arms sales and the military assistance to the Contras.

As a result of Walsh's investigations, North and Poindexter

were convicted on charges of obstructing justice and related offenses. Their convictions were overturned on appeal, however, on the grounds that testimony given at their trials had been influenced by information they had supplied to Congress under a limited grant of immunity.

Reagan accepted responsibility for the arms-for-hostages deal but denied any knowledge of the diversion. Although no evidence came to light to indicate that he was more deeply involved, many in Congress and the public remained skeptical. Nevertheless, most of the public eventually appeared willing to forgive him for whatever they thought he had done, and his popularity, which had dropped dramatically during the first months of the crisis, gradually recovered.

In retrospect, the Iran-Contra Affair was another skirmish in the struggle between the executive and legislative branches over the conduct of foreign policy. Reagan and his advisers evidently believed, in light of the changed mood of the country after 1980 and his own electoral landslides, that they could revive the sort of vigorous intelligence and covert activities that the executive branch had engaged in before the Vietnam War and the Watergate scandal.

The Democrats, who controlled both houses of Congress again after 1986, argued that covert operations subverted the separation of powers and the U.S. Constitution. The Iran-Contra Affair was especially odious, in their view, because it contradicted the express policy not to deal with terrorists or governments that harbored them. The administration's defenders retorted that the United States would be impotent to combat terrorism and espionage without strong and secret counterintelligence capabilities and that, since the Congress had effectively hamstrung the CIA and too often leaked news of its activities, personnel of the NSC had taken matters into their own hands. The proper roles of the branches of the U.S. government in the formulation and execution of foreign policy thus remained a major source of bitterness and confusion after almost half a century of American leadership in global politics.

Iran Hostage Crisis

Iran's revolution of 1978–1979 deeply altered that country's relationship with the United States. Iran's deposed ruler, Mohammad Reza Shah Pahlavi, had been close to a succession of U.S. administrations, but this had produced deep suspicion and hostility among Iran's revolutionary leaders, from both the left and the right of the political spectrum. Beginning in the fall of 1978, the U.S. embassy in Tehran had been the scene of frequent demonstrations by Iranians who opposed the American presence in the country, and on February 14, 1979, about a month after the shah had fled Iran, the embassy was attacked and briefly occupied. The embassy weathered this

Blindfolded American hostages are paraded for the Iranian public;
November 5, 1979.

assault, during which several embassy personnel were killed or wounded, but Iran was in the throes of enormous revolutionary change, which called for a new U.S. posture in Iran. Consequently, by the start of the hostage crisis the embassy staff had been cut from more than 1,400 personnel before the revolution to about 70 men and women. In addition, attempts had been made to arrive at a modus vivendi with Iran's provisional government, and during the spring and summer the Iranian authorities sought to strengthen security around the embassy complex.

In October 1979 the U.S. State Department was informed that the deposed Iranian monarch required medical treatment his aides claimed was available only in the United States; U.S. authorities, in turn, informed Iranian Prime Minister Mehdi Bazargan of the shah's impending arrival on American soil. Bazargan, in light of the February attack, guaranteed the safety of the U.S. embassy and its staff. The shah arrived in New York on October 22. The initial public response in Iran was moderate, but on November 4 the embassy was attacked by a mob of perhaps 3,000, some of whom were armed and who, after a short siege, took 63 American men and women hostage. (An additional three members of the diplomatic staff were taken hostage at the Iranian Foreign Ministry.) Attempts within the next few days by representatives of U.S. President Jimmy Carter (and by Tehran-based diplomats from other countries, alarmed at this breach of international protocol) to free the hostages failed. An American delegation headed by former U.S. Attorney General Ramsey Clark—who had long relations with many Iranian officials—was refused admission to Iran.

A political struggle was afoot in Tehran—between the Islamic right and secular left, and between various personalities within the Muslim coterie surrounding the revolutionary leader Ayatollah Ruhollah Khomeini—and the hostages apparently were caught in the gridlock. It soon became evident that no one within the virulently anti-American atmosphere of post revolutionary Iran was willing, or able, to expend the political capital necessary to effect the release of the hostages. The hostage-takers themselves were apparently supporters of Khomeini—whose failure to order the release of the hostages led Bazargan to resign on November 6—and demanded, as a condition of the hostages' release, that the United States extradite the shah to Iran.

On November 12, acting Iranian Foreign Minister Abolhasan Bani-Sadr indicated that the hostages would be released on three conditions: that the United States cease interfering in Iranian affairs, that the shah be returned to Iran for trial, and that those assets currently in the possession of the shah be declared stolen property. The United States responded by stating that U.S. courts would be open for Iran to make any financial claims it desired against the shah and further declared that it would support the establishment of an international commission to investigate purported human rights abuses under the shah's former regime. As a precondition of any such actions, however, the hostages would have to be returned.

The United States bolstered its position by refusing to purchase Iranian oil, by freezing billions of dollars of Iranian assets in the United States, and by engaging throughout the crisis in a vigorous campaign of international diplomacy against the Iranians. U.S. diplomats twice obtained United Nations (UN) Security Council resolutions (on December 4 and 31) against Iran's actions, and on November 29 the United States filed suit against the Iranian government in the International Court of Justice (which ruled in favor of the United States in May 1980). The consensus of the international community was against the Iranian seizure of the hostages, and diplomats from various countries sought to intervene on their behalf. In fact, on January 28, 1980, six American diplomats who had managed to avoid capture fled Iran with the help of diplomats from the Canadian embassy (which was subsequently closed).

Earlier, on November 17, Khomeini had ordered the release of 13 hostages, all women or African Americans, on the grounds that they were unlikely to be spies (another hostage, who became gravely ill, was released on July 11, 1980, leaving the number of hostages at 52), and, in fact, the threat that the hostages would be put on trial for various crimes, including espionage, was leverage that the Iranians used throughout the ordeal.

Almost from the beginning, U.S. military forces had begun to formulate plans to recover the hostages, and by early April 1980 the U.S. administration, still unable to find anyone to negotiate with in a meaningful fashion, sought a military option. Despite political turbulence in Iran, the hostages were still being held by their original captors in the embassy complex. On April 24, a small U.S. task force landed in the desert southeast of Tehran. From that staging point, a group of special operations soldiers was to advance via helicopter to a second rally point, stage a quick raid of the embassy compound, and convey the hostages to an airstrip that was to be secured beforehand by a second team of soldiers who were to fly directly from outside Iran. The soldiers and hostages would then withdraw by air. The operation was fraught with problems from the beginning. Two of the eight helicopters sent for the operation suffered malfunctions before arriving at the first staging area and another broke down on the site. Unable to complete their mission, U.S. forces sought to withdraw, during which one of the remaining helicopters collided with a support aircraft. Eight U.S. service members were killed, and their bodies, left behind, were paraded before Iranian television cameras. The Carter administration, humiliated by the failed mission and loss of life, expended great energy to have bodies returned to the United States. Secretary of State Cyrus Vance, who had opposed the mission, resigned in protest. All diplomatic initiatives in the hostage crises came to a standstill, and the hostages were placed, incommunicado, in new, concealed locations.

By May 1980, the United States had convinced its closest allies to institute an economic embargo of Iran. However, the embargo alone was not enough to weaken Iranian resolve vis-à-vis the hostage situation; nor, for that matter, did the shah's death on July 27 resolve the dilemma. Two subsequent events, however, made a resolution of the crisis seem more likely. First, in mid-August Iran finally installed a new government, and the Carter administration immediately sought to extend diplomatic overtures. Second, on September 22 Iraq invaded Iran. Although the Iran-Iraq War (1980–1990) distracted Iranian officials from hostage negotiations in the short term, the embargo continued to wear away at the Iranian economy and the country's ability to stave off Iraqi forces. Likewise, numerous world leaders made it clear to Iranian Prime Minister Mohammad Ali Raja'i, when he visited the UN in October, that Iran could not expect support in the Iraq conflict as long as it held the U.S. hostages.

As a consequence, Iranian officials engaged in negotiations with a new vigor. Raja'i insisted that there be no direct negotiations, however, and Algerian diplomats acted as middlemen throughout the remainder of the process. Negotiations continued throughout late 1980 and early 1981, during which time the Iranian demands centered largely on releasing frozen Iranian assets and lifting the trade embargo. An agreement having been made, the hostages were released on January 20, 1981, minutes after the inauguration of the new U.S. president, Ronald Reagan.

The Iran Hostage Crisis was a severe blow to U.S. morale and prestige, coming as it did in the aftermath of the Vietnam War. The crisis was to place a roadblock in the path of U.S.-Iranian relations for decades to come. It was also widely believed that the crisis contributed to Carter's defeat by Reagan in the 1980 presidential election. Moreover, in the years following the crisis, allegations arose that the Reagan campaign camp had acted to hinder the attempts by Carter to negotiate an earlier settlement—thus derailing a possible electoral coup for the Carter campaign—in an effort to ensure a Reagan victory. Although that contention has been largely dismissed, questions have remained about the willingness of officials in the Reagan administration to trade arms with the Iranians in the mid-1980s, in what became known as the Iran-Contra Affair.

Iran-Iraq War

The Iran-Iraq War began on September 22, 1980, when Iraqi armed forces invaded western Iran along the countries' joint border. The roots of the war lay in a number of territorial and political disputes between Iraq and Iran. Iraq wanted to seize control of the rich oil-producing Iranian border region of Khuzestan, a territory inhabited largely by ethnic Arabs over which Iraq sought to extend some form of suzerainty. Iraqi President Saddam Hussein wanted to reassert his country's

Iraqi troops construct a floating bridge near Khorramshahr, Iran, during the Iran-Iraq War, 1981.

sovereignty over both banks of the Shatt al-Arab, a river formed by the confluence of the Tigris and Euphrates rivers that was historically the border between the two countries. Saddam was also concerned over attempts by Iran's Islamic revolutionary government to incite rebellion among Iraq's Shi'ite majority. By attacking when it did, Iraq took advantage of the apparent disorder and isolation of Iran's new government—then at loggerheads with the United States over the seizure of the U.S. embassy in Tehran and its staff by Iranian militants—and of the demoralization and dissolution of Iran's regular armed forces.

In September 1980 the Iraqi army carefully advanced along a broad front into Khuzestan, taking Iran by surprise. Iraq's troops captured the city of Khorramshahr but failed to take the important oil-refining center of Abadan, and by December 1980 the Iraqi offensive had bogged down about 50 to 75 miles inside Iran after meeting unexpectedly strong Iranian resistance. Iran's counterattacks using the revolutionary militia (Revolutionary Guards) to bolster its regular armed forces began to compel the Iraqis to give ground in 1981. The Iranians first pushed the Iraqis back across Iran's Karun River and then recaptured Khorramshahr in 1982. Later that year Iraq voluntarily withdrew its forces from all captured Iranian territory and began seeking a peace agreement with Iran. But under the leadership of Ayatollah Ruhollah Khomeini, who bore a strong personal animosity toward Saddam, Iran remained intransigent and continued the war in an effort to overthrow the Iraqi leader. Iraq's defenses solidified once its troops were defending their own soil, and the war settled into a stalemate with a static, entrenched front running just inside and along Iraq's border. Iran repeatedly launched fruitless infantry attacks, using human assault waves composed partly of untrained and unarmed conscripts (often young boys snatched from the streets), which were repelled by the superior firepower and airpower of the Iraqis. Both nations engaged in sporadic air and missile attacks against each other's cities and military and oil installations. They also attacked each other's oil-tanker shipping in the Persian Gulf, and Iran's attacks on Kuwait's and other Gulf states' tankers prompted the United States and several Western European nations to station warships in the Persian Gulf to ensure the flow of oil to the rest of the world.

The oil-exporting capacity of both nations was severely reduced at various times owing to air strikes and to pipeline shutoffs, and the consequent reduction in their income and foreign-currency earnings brought the countries' economic development programs to a near standstill. Iraq's war effort was openly financed by Saudi Arabia, Kuwait, and other neighboring Arab states and was tacitly supported by the United States and the Soviet Union, while Iran's only major allies were Syria and Libya. Iraq continued to sue for peace in the mid-1980s, but its international reputation was damaged by reports that it had used lethal chemical weapons against Iranian troops as well as against Iraqi-Kurdish civilians, whom the Iraqi government thought to be sympathetic to Iran. (One such attack, in and around the Kurdish village of Halabjah in March 1988, killed as many as 5,000 civilians.) In the mid-1980s the military stalemate continued, but in August 1988 Iran's deteriorating economy and recent Iraqi gains on the battlefield compelled Iran to accept a United Nations–mediated cease-fire that it had previously resisted.

The total number of combatants on both sides is unclear; but both countries were fully mobilized, and most men of military age were under arms. The number of casualties was enormous but equally uncertain. Estimates of total casualties range from 1 million to twice that number. The number killed on both sides was perhaps 500,000, with Iran suffering the greater losses. Some 100,000 Kurds were killed by Iraqi forces during the final months of the war.

In August–September 1990, while Iraq was preoccupied with its invasion of Kuwait, Iraq and Iran restored diplomatic relations, and Iraq agreed to Iranian terms for the settlement of the war: the withdrawal of Iraqi troops from occupied Iranian territory, division of sovereignty over the Shatt al-Arab waterway, and a prisoner-of-war exchange. The final exchange of prisoners was not completed until March 2003.

Iraq: "Operation Iraqi Freedom"

Often termed the Second Persian Gulf War or the Iraq War, this was a brief conflict in 2003 between Iraq and a combined force of troops from the United States and Great Britain, with smaller contingents from several other countries. The war led to the rapid defeat of Iraqi military and paramilitary forces and the occupation of Iraq.

Prelude to War

Iraq's invasion of Kuwait in 1990 ended in Iraq's defeat by a U.S.-led coalition in the First Persian Gulf War (1990–1991). However, the Iraqi branch of the Ba'th Party, headed by Saddam Hussein, managed to retain power by harshly suppressing uprisings of the country's minority Kurds and its majority

U.S. soldier plots the location of friendly forces near Baghdad, Iraq, 2005.

Shi'ite Arabs. To stem the exodus of Kurds from Iraq, the allies established a "safe haven" in northern Iraq's predominantly Kurdish regions, and allied warplanes patrolled "no fly" zones in northern and southern Iraq that were off-limits to Iraqi aircraft. Moreover, to restrain future Iraqi aggression, the United Nations (UN) implemented economic sanctions against Iraq in order to, among other things, hinder the progress of its most lethal arms programs, including those for the development of nuclear, biological, and chemical weapons. UN inspections during the mid-1990s uncovered a variety of proscribed weapons and prohibited technology throughout Iraq. That country's continued flouting of the UN weapons ban and its repeated interference with the inspections frustrated the international community and led U.S. President Bill Clinton in 1998 to order the bombing of several Iraqi military installations (Operation Desert Fox). After the bombing, however, Iraq refused to allow inspectors to reenter the country, and during the next several years the economic sanctions slowly began to erode as neighboring countries sought to reopen trade with Iraq.

In 2002 the new U.S. president, George W. Bush, argued that the vulnerability of the United States following the September 11 attacks of 2001, combined with Iraq's alleged continued possession and manufacture of weapons of mass destruction and its support for terrorist groups—which, according to the Bush administration, included al-Qaeda, the perpetrators of the September 11 attacks—made the disarming of Iraq a renewed priority. UN Security Council Resolution 1441, passed on November 8, 2002, demanded that Iraq readmit inspectors and that it comply with all previous resolutions. Iraq complied with the resolution, but in early 2003 President Bush and British Prime Minister Tony Blair declared that Iraq was continuing to hinder UN inspections and that it retained proscribed weapons. Other world leaders, such as French President Jacques Chirac and German Chancellor Gerhard Schröder, citing what they believed to be increased Iraqi cooperation, sought to extend inspections and give Iraq more time to comply with them.

However, on March 17, seeking no further UN resolutions and deeming further diplomatic efforts by the Security Council futile, Bush declared an end to diplomacy and issued an ultimatum to Saddam, giving the Iraqi president 48 hours to leave Iraq. The leaders of France, Germany, and Russia, among others, saw this hastening to war as unnecessary belligerence.

The Conflict

When Saddam refused to leave Iraq, U.S. and allied forces launched an attack on March 20 at 5:34 AM (local time) that began when U.S. aircraft dropped several precision-guided bombs on a bunker complex in which the Iraqi president was believed to be meeting with senior staff. This attack was followed by a series of air strikes directed against government and military installations, and within days U.S. forces had invaded Iraq from Kuwait in the south (U.S. Special Forces had previously been deployed to Kurdish-controlled areas in the north). Despite fears that Iraqi forces would engage in a scorched-earth policy—destroying bridges and dams and setting fire to Iraq's

U.S. soldiers prepare to clear a building near Iskandariyyah, Iraq, 2005.

southern oil wells—little damage was done by retreating Iraqi forces; in fact, large numbers of Iraqi troops simply chose not to resist the advance of coalition forces. In southern Iraq the greatest resistance for U.S. forces as they advanced northward was from irregular groups of Ba'th Party supporters, known as Saddam's Fedayeen. British forces—which had deployed around the southern city of Al-Basrah—faced similar resistance from paramilitary and irregular fighters.

In central Iraq, units of the Republican Guard—a heavily armed paramilitary group connected with the ruling party—were deployed to defend the capital of Baghdad. As U.S. Army and Marine Corps forces advanced northwestward up the Tigris-Euphrates river valley, they bypassed many populated areas where Fedayeen resistance was strongest and were slowed only on March 25 when inclement weather and a sorely stretched supply line briefly forced them to halt their advance within 60 miles (95 km) of Baghdad. During the pause, U.S. aircraft inflicted heavy damage on Republican Guard units around the capital. U.S. forces resumed their advance within a week, and on April 4 they took control of Baghdad's international airport. Iraqi resistance, though at times vigorous, was highly disorganized, and over the next several days U.S. Army and Marine Corps units staged raids into the heart of the city. On April 9 resistance in Baghdad collapsed, and U.S. soldiers took control of the city.

On that same day Al-Basrah was finally secured by British forces, which had entered the city several days earlier. In the north, however, plans to open up another major front had been frustrated when the Turkish government refused to allow mechanized and armored U.S. Army units to pass through Turkey to deploy in northern Iraq. Regardless, a regiment of American paratroopers did drop into the area, and U.S. Special Forces soldiers joined with Kurdish *peshmerga* fighters to seize the northern cities of Kirkuk on April 10 and Mosul on April 11. Saddam's hometown of Tikrit, the last major stronghold of the regime, fell with little resistance on April 13. Isolated groups of regime loyalists continued to fight in subsequent days, but the U.S. president declared an end to major combat on May 1. Iraqi leaders fled into hiding, only to be tracked down by U.S. forces. Saddam Hussein was captured on December 13, 2003, and was turned over to Iraqi authorities in June 2004 to stand trial for various crimes.

The Aftermath

Following the collapse of the Ba'thist regime, Iraq's major cities erupted in a wave of looting that was directed mostly at government offices and other public institutions, and there were severe outbreaks of violence—both common criminal violence and acts of reprisal against the former ruling clique. Restoring law and order was one of the most arduous tasks for the occupying forces, one that was exacerbated by continued attacks against occupying troops that soon developed into a full-scale guerrilla war. Coalition combat casualties had been light, with about 150 deaths by May 1, 2003. But American casualties soared to some 1,000, as a result of postwar guerrilla activity by the time of the

Results of a car-bomb explosion at a police station in Baghdad, Iraq, 2004.

U.S. presidential election of November 2004. Though the exact number is uncertain, thousands of Iraqi soldiers and civilians may have died during the war.

After 35 years of Ba'thist rule that included three major wars and a dozen years of economic sanctions, the economy was in shambles and only slowly began to recover. Moreover, the country remained saddled with a ponderous debt that vastly exceeded its annual gross domestic product, and oil production—the country's single greatest source of revenue— was badly hobbled. The continuing guerrilla assaults on occupying forces and leaders of the new Iraqi government in the year after the war only compounded the difficulty of rebuilding Iraq.

In the Shi'ite regions of southern Iraq, many of the local religious leaders (ayatollahs) who had fled Saddam's regime returned to the country, and Shi'ites from throughout the world were able to resume pilgrimage to the holy cities of Al-Najaf and Karbala that had been banned under Saddam. Throughout the country Iraqis began the painful task of seeking loved ones who had fallen victim to the former regime; mass graves, the result of numerous government pogroms over the years, yielded thousands of victims.

A Controversial War

Unlike the common consent reached in the First Persian Gulf War, no broad coalition was assembled to remove Saddam and his Ba'th Party from power. Although some European leaders voiced their conditional support for the war and none regretted the end of the violent Ba'thist regime, public opinion in Europe and the Middle East was overwhelmingly against the war. Many in the Middle East saw it as a new brand of anti-Arab and anti-Islamic imperialism, and most Arab leaders decried the occupation of a fellow Arab country by foreign troops. Reaction to the war was mixed in the United States. Though several antiwar protests occurred in American cities, many opinion polls showed considerable support for military action against Iraq before and during the war. Surprisingly, American opinions on the war sometimes crossed traditional party lines and doctrinal affiliation, with many to the right of the avowedly conservative Bush seeing the war as an act of reckless internationalism and some to the political left—appalled by the Ba'thist regime's brutal human rights violations and its consistent aggression— giving grudging support to military action.

As violence continued and casualties mounted, however, more Americans (including some who had initially supported the war) began to criticize the Bush administration for what they perceived to be the mishandling of postwar Iraq. The appearance in the news of photographs of U.S. soldiers abusing Iraqis at Abu Ghraib prison—a facility notorious for brutality under the Ba'th regime—further damaged world opinion of the United States. A U.S. bipartisan commission formed to investigate the September 11 attacks reported in July 2004 that though there were links between the Iraqi regime and al-Qaeda going back several years, there was no evidence of a "collaborative operational relationship" between them. Supporters of the war viewed this conclusion as vindication of the Bush administration's prewar assertions, while critics saw in the finding proof that the administration had overstated the connection between Iraq and al-Qaeda.

Bush's prewar claims, the failure of U.S. intelligence services to correctly gauge Iraq's weapons capacity, and the failure to find any weapons of mass destruction—the Bush administration's primary reason for going to war—became major political debating points. The war, not surprisingly, was a central issue of the 2004 U.S. presidential election.

Warfare in the 21st Century

by Peter Saracino

The war that began in Afghanistan, Iran's eastern neighbor, on October 7, 2001, demonstrated both the capabilities and the limitations of modern military technology. It should have come as no surprise that the U.S.-led 17-member coalition toppled the Taliban regime in only a few weeks. In conventional terms, the Taliban were a pushover; they possessed no air force, had very limited air defenses, and were an unpopular and weak regime. It must be remembered, however, that in 1979 the Soviet Union controlled Afghanistan's capital, Kabul, within a week of beginning its invasion and then spent the next decade trying to defeat the mujahideen guerrillas. The coalition faced a similar challenge in 2002 against widely dispersed and tenacious Taliban and al-Qaeda forces operating in rugged and inhospitable terrain. Consequently, the coalition has yet to eliminate Afghanistan's guerrilla resistance or determine the fate of al-Qaeda leader Osama bin Laden.

New Weapons

Shortly after the war began, an American bomb designed to destroy underground tunnels and bunkers was rushed into service. The BLU-118/B thermobaric bomb was dropped on a suspected enemy cave in the eastern part of the country in March 2002. Although the device detonated as intended, a problem with its laser guidance caused it to land far enough away from the cave entrance to negate its effect. Thermobaric weapons work in two stages: first they release a fine cloud of high-explosive fuel, and then the fuel is detonated, creating a large fireball and a devastating shock wave. These weapons are most effective in confined spaces, because there the immense overpressures they create are contained and magnified. Ironically, the Soviets employed thermobaric bombs in Afghanistan in the 1980s. Research on thermobaric bombs continues in the United States, the United Kingdom, and other countries as a means of destroying deep underground bunkers and hidden supplies of biological or chemical weapons without having to resort to the use of tactical nuclear weapons.

Another device, the laser-guided bomb, now used by many countries, has two main disadvantages: the laser beam marking the target has to be aimed by someone on the ground or from a nearby aircraft, and smoke and bad weather can degrade the laser beam so that it is not able to guide the falling bomb. In Afghanistan such problems were overcome through the use of the new Global Positioning System (GPS) Aided Munition. A computer mounted in the bomb is programmed with the coordinates of the intended target and uses GPS guidance to strike with a reported accuracy of 40 to 60 feet. Since the First Persian Gulf War (1990–1991), special forces troops have been using handheld GPS receivers, laser designators, and satellite radios to help artillery and aircraft attack targets with minimal delay. This capability has assumed a greater importance in Afghanistan, where reducing the "sensor to shooter" loop to just a few minutes has helped pin down and destroy small groups of guerrillas on the move.

The Afghan War will also be remembered as the first in which armed unmanned aerial vehicles (UAVs) were used to attack targets. UAVs have been in service for more than 40 years as drones for target practice and to gather intelligence with onboard sensors, but the U.S. Central Intelligence Agency used a specially adapted Predator UAV to fire a Hellfire antitank missile at a group of three men believed to be al-Qaeda leaders. All were killed, but it later turned out that they were local villagers. Although expensive (the price of a Global Hawk UAV is more than $15 million, and a Predator costs in excess of $3.3 million), they have the advantage of being able to fly over enemy territory without risking the lives of pilots and can remain on patrol longer than most manned aircraft. UAVs are, however, vulnerable to ground fire, bad weather, ice buildup on their wings, and operator error.

Logistic Challenges

One thing that sets the U.S. military apart from all others is its ability to dispatch thousands of troops and their weapons, vehicles, and supplies to any point on Earth and to sustain them there. No other country could wage war in a landlocked country such as Afghanistan while supplying its forces almost entirely by air. By the end of September 2001, nearly the entire active-duty fleet of U.S. C-5 Galaxy and C-17 Globemaster III transport aircraft—a total of about 140 aircraft—was dedicated to the war effort. The 30-year-old C-5 can carry 270,000 pounds of cargo, but it requires a runway at least 4,900 feet long for landing. Conversely, the C-17 can land on runways as short as 3,000 feet, which makes it much better suited to the primitive or war-damaged airfields in Afghanistan. At the height of the war in early 2002, coalition troops each month consumed 2.1 million gallons of fuel, 3.6 million gallons of water, and the equivalent of 72 18-wheel transport trucks of food. Meeting such a demand for supplies does not come cheap, however. For example, the price of delivering fuel to remote war zones can exceed $400 per gallon.

The Role of Special Forces

The elimination of remaining al-Qaeda and Taliban members from their isolated mountain caves and village hideouts has remained problematic for the coalition and is a major reason why up to 2,000 special forces troops have been committed to the campaign. Although much of their work has been kept secret, several coalition members have admitted that they have deployed such forces, including Australia, Canada, Denmark, Germany, Norway, Turkey, the United Kingdom, and the United States. What sets special operations forces apart from regular troops is that they tend to be organized in groups of fewer than a dozen soldiers and are trained in specialties such as mountain, desert, and jungle warfare, counterterrorism, combat search-and-rescue operations, and covert reconnaissance. Special forces troops are also highly mobile and take advantage of specialized equipment that permits them to travel at night and in most weather conditions. For example, the MH-53J Pave Low III heavy-lift helicopter (based on the 1960s-era CH-53 Sea Stallion) has sophisticated radar and a forward-looking infrared sensor to enable its crew to avoid obstacles and fly just above the ground at night. The Pave Low is equipped with armor plating and machine guns and can transport up to 38 troops.

Command and Information

For the most part, the war in Afghanistan has been managed from U.S. Central Command (CENTCOM) headquarters in Florida, more than 7,000 miles and 10 time zones away. The CENTCOM area of responsibility reaches from the horn of Africa in the southwest to the countries of Central Asia in the northeast, a region in which Iran rests at the very center. Commanders at CENTCOM headquarters have for the first time been able to watch battles live via TV cameras mounted in UAVs. Although a technical achievement, this has led to complaints that the attention of headquarters staff is diverted and that troops in the field are being micromanaged. The large volume of data moving between commanders and troops in the field has been a mixed blessing for coalition forces. On one hand it has allowed commanders to deploy forces quickly and effectively to where they are needed most, but on the other hand information overload has created the requirement for new positions, such as that of "knowledge management officer" to filter out minor details and ensure that commanders get only the information they need to make decisions.

Peter Saracino is a freelance defense journalist and a contributor to PEJ News based in Victoria, B.C., Canada.

The Islamic Revolution (1978–1979)

Prelude to Revolution

Petroleum revenues continued to fuel Iran's economy in the 1970s, and in 1973 Iran concluded a new 20-year oil agreement with a consortium of Western firms led by British Petroleum (formerly Anglo-Iranian Oil). This agreement gave direct control of Iranian oil fields to the government under the auspices of the National Iranian Oil Company (NIOC) and initiated a standard seller-buyer relationship between the NIOC and the oil companies. Mohammad Reza Shah was acutely aware of the danger of depending on a diminishing oil asset and pursued a policy of economic diversification. Iran had begun automobile production in the 1950s and by the early 1970s was exporting motor vehicles to Egypt and Yugoslavia. The government exploited the country's copper reserves, and in 1972 Iran's first steel mill began producing structural steel. Iran also invested heavily overseas and continued to press for barter agreements for the marketing of its petroleum and natural gas.

This apparent success, however, veiled deep-seated problems. World monetary instability and fluctuations in Western oil consumption seriously threatened an economy that had been rapidly expanding since the early 1950s and that was still directed on a vast scale toward high-cost development programs and large military expenditures. A decade of extraordinary economic growth, heavy government spending, and a boom in oil prices led to high rates of inflation, and—despite an elevated level of employment, held artificially high by loans and credits— the buying power of Iranians and their overall standard of living stagnated. Prices skyrocketed as supply failed to keep up with demand, and a 1975 government-sponsored war on high prices resulted in arrests and fines of traders and manufacturers, injuring confidence in the market. The agricultural sector, poorly managed in the years since land reform, continued to decline in productivity.

The shah's reforms also had failed completely to provide any degree of political participation. The sole political outlet within Iran was the rubber-stamp Majles, dominated since the time of Mohammad Mosaddeq by two parties, both of which were subservient to and sponsored by the shah. Traditional parties such as the National Front had been marginalized, while others, such as the Communist Tudeh Party, were outlawed and forced to operate covertly. Protest all too often took the form of subversive and violent activity by groups such as the Mojahedin-e Khalq and Feda'iyan-e Khalq, organizations with both Marxist and religious tendencies. All forms of social and political protest, either from the intellectual left or the religious right, were subject to censorship, surveillance, or harassment by the shah's secret police, SAVAK, and illegal detention and torture were common.

Many argued that since Iran's brief experiment with parliamentary democracy and Communist politics had failed, the country had to go back to its indigenous culture. The 1953 coup against Mosaddeq had particularly incensed the intellectuals. For the first time in more than half a century, the secular intellectuals, many of whom were fascinated by the populist appeal of Ayatollah Ruhollah Khomeini, abandoned their project of reducing the authority and power of the Shi'ite 'ulama' (religious scholars) and argued that with the help of the 'ulama', the shah could be overthrown.

In this environment, members of the National Front, the Tudeh Party, and their various splinter groups now joined the 'ulama' in a broad opposition to the shah's regime. Khomeini had continued to preach in exile about the evils of the Pahlavi regime, accusing the shah of irreligion and subservience to foreign powers. Thousands of tapes and print copies of the ayatollah's speeches were smuggled into Iran during the 1970s as an increasing number of unemployed and working-poor Iranians—mostly new immigrants from the countryside who were disenchanted by the cultural vacuum of modern urban Iran—turned to the *'ulama'* for guidance. The shah's dependence on the United States, his close ties with Israel—then engaged in extended hostilities with the overwhelmingly Muslim Arab states—and his regime's ill-considered economic policies served to fuel the potency of dissident rhetoric with the masses.

Revolution

Outwardly, with a swiftly expanding economy and a rapidly modernizing infrastructure, everything was going well in Iran. But in little more than a generation, Iran had changed from a traditional, conservative, and rural society to one that was industrial, modern, and urban. The sense that in both agriculture and industry too much had been attempted too soon and that the government, either through corruption or incompetence, had failed to deliver all that was promised was manifested in demonstrations against the regime in 1978.

In January 1978, incensed by what they considered to be slanderous remarks made against exiled spiritual leader Ruhollah Khomeini in a Tehran newspaper, thousands of young *madrasah* students took to the streets. They were followed by thousands more Iranian youth—mostly unemployed recent immigrants from the countryside—who began protesting the regime's excesses. The shah, weakened by cancer and stunned by the sudden outpouring of hostility against him, vacillated, assuming the protests to be part of an international conspiracy against him. Many people were killed by government forces in the ensuing chaos, serving only to fuel the violence in a Shi'ite country where martyrdom played a fundamental role in religious expression. Despite all government efforts, a cycle of violence began in which each death fueled further protest, and all protest—from the secular left and religious right—became subsumed under the cloak of Shi'ite Islam.

During his exile, Khomeini coordinated this upsurge of opposition—first from Iraq and after 1978 from France—demanding the shah's abdication. In January 1979, in what was officially described as a "vacation," the shah and his family fled Iran; he died the following year in Cairo.

The Regency Council established to run the country during the shah's absence proved unable to function, and Prime Minister Shahpur Bakhtiar, hastily appointed by the shah before his departure, was incapable of effecting compromise with either his former National Front colleagues or Khomeini. Crowds in excess of a million demonstrated in Tehran, proving the wide appeal of Khomeini, who arrived in Iran amid wild rejoicing on February 1. Ten days later Bakhtiar went into hiding, eventually to find exile in France, where he was assassinated in 1991.

On April 1, following overwhelming support in a national referendum, Khomeini declared Iran an Islamic republic. Elements within the clergy promptly moved to exclude their former left-wing, nationalist, and intellectual allies from any positions of power in the new regime, and a return to conservative social values was enforced. The Family Protection Act, which provided further guarantees and rights to women in marriage, was declared void, and mosque-based revolutionary bands known as *komiteh*s (Persian "committees") patrolled the streets enforcing Islamic codes of dress and behavior and dispatching impromptu justice to perceived enemies of the revolution. Throughout most of 1979 the Revolutionary Guards—then an informal religious militia formed by Khomeini to forestall another CIA-backed coup, as in the days of Mosaddeq—engaged in similar activity, aimed at intimidating and repressing political groups not under control of the ruling Revolutionary Council and its sister Islamic Republican Party, both clerical organizations loyal to Khomeini. The violence and brutality often exceeded those of SAVAK under the shah.

The militias and the clerics they supported made every effort to suppress Western cultural influence, and, facing persecution and violence, many of the Western-educated elite fled the country. This anti-Western sentiment eventually manifested itself in the November 1979 seizure of the U.S. embassy by a group of Iranian protesters demanding the extradition of the shah, who at that time was undergoing medical treatment in the United States. Through the embassy takeover, Khomeini's supporters could claim to be as "anti-imperialist" as the political left. This ultimately gave them the ability to suppress most of the regime's left-wing and moderate opponents. The Assembly of Experts (the Majles-e Khobregan), overwhelmingly dominated by clergy, ratified a new constitution the following month. Taking 66 U.S. citizens hostage at their embassy and at the Iranian Foreign Ministry proved to highlight the fractures that had begun to occur within the revolutionary regime itself. Moderates, such as provisional Prime Minister Mehdi Bazargan and the republic's first president, Abolhasan Bani-Sadr, who opposed holding the hostages, were steadily forced from power by conservatives within the government who questioned their revolutionary zeal.

The Islamic World

Adherence to Islam is a global phenomenon: Muslims predominate in some 50 countries and form significant minorities in dozens more, including some Western European countries. The area of significant Muslim habitation extends from the Atlantic to the Pacific and along a belt that stretches across northern and central Africa into Central Asia and south to the northern regions of the Indian subcontinent and the archipelago countries of Indonesia, Malaysia, and the Philippines. Arabs, the ethnic group that was the original professor of Islam, now account for fewer than one-fifth of all Muslims. Despite the absence of large-scale Islamic political entities of earlier periods—such the various empires and dynasties that dominated the region—the Islamic faith continues to expand, by some estimates faster than any other major religion.

The history of the Muslims in modern times has often been explained in terms of the impact of the "West." From this perspective, the 18th century in the Islamic world was a period of degeneration and a prelude to European domination. By the 18th century one particular set of societies in Western Europe had developed an economic and social system capable of transcending the 5,000-year-old limitations of the agrarian-based settled world as defined by the Greeks (who called it Oikoumene). European explorers had built on and surpassed Muslim seafaring technology to compete in the southern seas and discover new sea routes—and, accidentally, a new source of wealth in the Americas. Moreover, European society developed a pattern in which the adoption of technological change came to be accepted and embraced. Europe's technology, however, could not easily be diffused to societies that had not undergone the prerequisite fundamental social and economic changes. Outside of Europe, gradual assimilation of the "new," which had characterized change and cultural diffusion for 5,000 years, had to be replaced by hurried imitation, which proved enormously disorienting. This combination of innovation and imitation produced an unprecedented and persisting imbalance among various parts of the Oikoumene. Muslims' responses paralleled those of other "non-Western" peoples but were often filtered through and expressed in peculiarly Islamic symbols and motifs. The power of Islam as a source of public values already had waxed and waned many times throughout the centuries; it intensified anew in the 18th and 19th centuries, receded in the early 20th century, and surged again after the mid-20th century.

From the mid-17th century through the 18th and early 19th centuries certain Muslims expressed an awareness of internal weakness. In some areas, Muslims were largely unaware of the rise of Europe; in others, such as India, Sumatra, and Java, the 18th century actually brought European control. Internal Muslim responses to decline, sometimes official and sometimes unofficial, sometimes Islamizing, sometimes Westernizing, fell into two categories, as the following examples demonstrate.

In some areas, leaders attempted to revive existing political systems. In Iran, for example, attempts at restoration combined military and religious reform. In about 1730 a Turk from Khorasan named Nadr Qoli Beg reorganized the Safavid army in the name of the Safavid shah, whom he replaced with himself in 1736. Nadir Shah, as he then styled himself, extended the borders of the Safavid state farther than ever; he even defeated the Ottoman Empire and may have been aspiring to be the leader of all Muslims. To this end he made overtures to neighboring rulers, seeking their recognition by trying to represent Iranian Shi'ism as a *madhhab* (legal school) alongside the Sunni *madhhab*s. After he was killed in 1747, however, his reforms did not survive and his house disintegrated. Karim Khan Zand, a general from Shiraz, ruled in the name of the Safavids but did not restore real power to the shah. By the time the Qajar dynasty (1779–1925) managed to again secure Iran's borders, reviving Safavid legitimacy was impossible.

In the Ottoman Empire, restoration involved selective imitation of things European. In its first phase, from 1718 to 1730 (known as the Tulip Period), experimentation with European manners and tastes was matched by experimentation with European military technology. Restoration depended on reinvigorating the military, the key to earlier Ottoman success, and Europeans were hired for the task. After Nadir Shah's defeat of the Ottoman army, this first phase of absolutist restoration ended, but the pursuit of European fashion had become a permanent element in Ottoman life. Meanwhile, central power continued to weaken, especially in the area of international commerce. The certificates of protection that had accompanied the Capitulations arrangements for foreign nationals were extended to non-Muslim Ottoman subjects, who gradually oriented themselves toward their foreign associates. The integration of such groups into the Ottoman state was further weakened by the recognition, in the disastrous Treaty of Küçük Kaynarca (1774), of the Russian tsar as protector of the Ottoman's Greek Orthodox *millet* (religious community). A second stage of absolutist restoration occurred under Selim III, who became sultan in the first year of the French Revolution and ruled until 1807. His military and political reforms, referred to as the New Order (Nizam-i Cedid), went beyond the Tulip Period in using things European. Here, as in Egypt under Muhammad 'Ali (reigned 1805–1848), the famed core of Janissaries that had been a source of Ottoman strength was destroyed and replaced with European-trained troops—a process the Safavids of Iran had experimented with nearly two centuries earlier.

In other areas, leaders envisioned or created new social orders that were self-consciously Islamic. The growing popularity of Westernization and a decreasing reliance on Islam as a source of public values was counterbalanced in many parts of the Islamic world by all sorts of Islamic activism, ranging from educational reform to jihad. "Islamic" politics often were marked by an oppositional quality that drew on long-standing traditions of skepticism about government. Sufism could play very different roles. In the form of renovated *tariqah*s (orders) it could support reform and stimulate pan-Islamic awareness. Sufis often encouraged the study of Hadith to establish the Prophet Muhammad as a model for spiritual and moral reconstruction and to invalidate many unacceptable traditional or customary Islamic practices. Sufi *tariqah*s provided interregional communication and contact and an indigenous form of social organization that could even lead to the founding of a dynasty, as in the case of the Libyan monarchy.

Sufism could also be condemned as a source of degeneracy. The most famous and influential militant anti-Sufi movement arose in the Arabian Peninsula and called itself the Muwahhidun ("Monotheists") but came to be known as Wahhabis, after its founder, Muhammad ibn 'Abd al-Wahhab (1703–1792). Inspired by the 14th-century Hanbali scholar Ibn Taymiyyah, 'Abd al-Wahhab argued that the Qur'an and sunnah (way of the Prophet) could provide the bases for a reconstruction of Islamic society out of the degenerate form in which it had come to be practiced. Islam itself was not an inhibiting force; "traditional" Islam was. Far from advocating the traditional, the Wahhabis argued that what had become traditional had strayed very far from the fundamental, which can always be found in the Qur'an and sunnah. The traditional they associated with blind imitation (*taqlid*); reform, with making the pious personal effort (*ijtihad*) necessary to understand the fundamentals. Within an Islamic context, this type of movement was not conservative, because it sought not to conserve what had been passed down but to renew what had been abandoned. The Wahhabi movement attracted the support of a tribe in the Najd led by Muhammad ibn Sa'ud. Although the first state produced by this alliance did not last, it laid the foundations for the existing Saudi state in Arabia and inspired similar activism elsewhere down to the present day.

In West Africa a series of activist movements appeared from the 18th century into the 19th. There as in Arabia, Islamic activism was directed less at non-Muslims than at Muslims who had gone astray. As in many of the Islamic world's outlying areas, emergent groups of indigenous educated, observant Muslims, such as the Tukulor of Senegal, were finding the casual, syncretistic, opportunistic nature of official Islam to be increasingly intolerable. Such Muslims were inspired by reformist scholars from numerous times and places; by a theory of jihad comparable to that of the Wahhabis; and by expectations of a *mujaddid* (renewer) as the Islamic century turned in AH 1200 (AD 1785). In what is now northern Nigeria, the discontent of the 1780s and '90s erupted in 1804, when Usman dan Fodio declared a jihad against the Hausa rulers. Jihad activity continued for a century; it again became millennial near the turn of the next Muslim century in AH 1300 (AD 1882), as the need to resist European occupation became more urgent. For example, Muhammad Ahmad declared himself to be the *mahdi* (messianic deliverer) in the Sudan in 1881.

In the Indian Ocean area, Islamic activism was more often intellectual and didactic. Its best exemplar was Shah Wali Allah of Delhi (1702–1762), the spiritual ancestor of many later Indian Muslim reform movements. During his lifetime the collapse of Muslim political power was painfully evident. He tried to unite the Muslims of India, not around Sufism, as Akbar had tried to do, but around Islamic canon law (Shari'ah). Like Ibn Taymiyyah, he understood the Shari'ah to be based on firm sources—Qur'an and sunnah—that could, with pious effort, be applied to present circumstances.

The many efforts to revive and resist change were largely unsuccessful. By 1818, British hegemony over India was complete; and many other colonies and mandates followed between then and the aftermath of World War I (1914–1918). Not all Muslim territories were colonized, but nearly all experienced some kind of dependency, be it psychological, political, techno-logical, cultural, or economic. Perhaps only the Saudi regime in the central parts of the Arabian Peninsula could be said to have escaped any kind of dependency; but even there oil exploration, begun in the 1930s, brought European interference. In the 19th century, Westernization and Islamic activism coexisted and competed. By the turn of the 20th century, secular ethnic nationalism had become the most common mode of protest in the Islamic world; but the spirit of Islamic reconstruction was also kept alive, either in conjunction with secular nationalism or in opposition to it.

In the 19th-century Ottoman Empire, selective Westernization coexisted with a reconsideration of Islam. The program of reform known as the Tanzimat, which was in effect from 1839 to 1876, aimed to emulate European law and administration by giving all Ottoman subjects, regardless of religious confession, equal legal standing and by limiting the powers of the monarch. In the 1860s a group known as the Young Ottomans tried to identify the basic principles of European liberalism and even love of nation with Islam itself. In Iran, the Qajar shahs brought in a special "Cossack Brigade," trained and led by Russians, while at the same time the Shi'ite *mujtahid*s viewed the decisions of their spiritual leader as binding on all Iranian Shi'ites and declared themselves to be independent of the shah. (One Shi'ite revolt, that of the Bab [died 1850], led to a whole new religion, the Baha'i faith.) Like the Young Ottomans, Shi'ite religious leaders came to identify with constitutionalism in opposition to the ruler.

Islamic protest often took the form of jihad against the Europeans: by Southeast Asians against the Dutch; by the Sanusi *tariqah* over Italian control in Libya; by the Mahdist movement in the Sudan; or by the Salihi *tariqah* in Somalia, led by Sayyid Muhammad ibn 'Abd Allah Hasan, who was tellingly nicknamed the Mad Mullah by the British. Sometimes religious leaders, like those of the Shi'ites in Iran, took part in constitutional revolutions (1905–1911). Underlying much of this activity was a pan-Islamic sentiment that drew on very old conceptions of the *ummah* (Islamic community) as the ultimate solidarity group for Muslims.

Three of the most prominent Islamic reconstructionists were Jamal al-Din al-Afghani (probably an Iranian Shi'ite, though he passed himself as an Afghan Sunni), his Egyptian disciple Muhammad 'Abduh, and the Indian poet Sir Muhammad Iqbal. All warned against blind pursuit of Westernization, arguing that the blame for the weaknesses of Muslims lay not with Islam, but rather with Muslims themselves, because they had lost touch with the progressive spirit of social, moral, and intellectual reconstruction that had made early Islamic civilization one of the greatest in human history. Although al-Afghani, who taught and preached throughout the Islamic world, acknowledged that organization by nationality might be necessary, he viewed it as inferior to Muslim identity. He further argued that Western technology could advance Muslims only if they retained and cultivated their own spiritual and cultural heritage. He pointed out that at one time Muslims had been intellectual and scientific leaders in the world, identifying a Golden Age under the 'Abbasid caliphate and pointing to the many contributions Muslims had made to the "West." Like al-Afghani, Iqbal assumed that without Islam Muslims could never regain the strength they had possessed when they were a vital force in the world, united in a single international community and unaffected by differences of language or ethnos.

This aggressive recovery of the past became a permanent theme of Islamic reconstruction. In many regions of the Islamic world the movement known as Salafiyyah also identified with an ideal time in history, that of the pious ancestors (salaf) in the early Muslim state of Muhammad and his companions, and advocated past-oriented change to bring present-day Muslims up to the progressive standards of an earlier ideal. In addition to clearly Islamic thinkers, there were others, such as the Egyptian Mustafa Kamil, whose nationalism was not simply secular. Kamil saw Egypt as simultaneously European, Ottoman, and Muslim. The Young Turk Revolution of 1908 was followed by a period in which similarly complex views of national identity were discussed in the Ottoman Empire.

Despite the ideological appeal of such positions, the need to throw off European control promoted the fortunes of secular nationalism and other narrower forms of loyalty. Especially after Japan's defeat of Russia in 1905, nationalist fervor increased. Sometimes it was associated with related ideologies, such as pan-Arabism, pan-Turkism, or Arab socialism. Many nationalists enthusiastically admired things European despite the fact that they were committed to resisting or removing European control. Often accepting European assessments of traditional religion as a barrier to modernization, many nationalists sought an identity in the pre-Islamic past.

Kemal Atatürk looked to the Turkic past in Central Asia and Anatolia to transform Ottomanism into a Turkish identity not dependent on Islam. "Islamic" dress was discouraged. Muslim males, who prayed with covered heads, were now asked to replace the fez, which could be kept on during prayer, with the brimmed hat, which could not. Arabic script, too closely associated with Islam, was replaced with the Latin.

In Iran, Reza Shah Pahlavi argued that the Islamic period was but an accidental interlude in the continuous history, since Achaemenid times, of Iran as a unified entity.

The Egyptian Taha Hussein connected his country's national identity with Pharaonic times and with Mediterranean–European culture; and therefore it could easily partake of modern Western civilization. Christians were thus as much Egyptians as were Muslims; the accompanying development of a standard literary Arabic, *fusha*, emphasized the unity of all Arabs, regardless of confession. These approaches allowed, indeed required, all religious communities to partake of a single legal and societal system.

Other nationalists made more of Islam. In Saudi Arabia and Pakistan, for example, Islam played a primary role in the formation of a national identity. In Pakistan it provided, according to the statesman Mohammed Ali Jinnah, an alternative for Muslims who would otherwise have to share in an identity defined by a Hindu majority. In many Arab countries, especially in North Africa, secular nationalism's downgrading of Islam was muted by a qualified acceptance of Islam as one, but not the only, important source of loyalty.

At the same time there were Muslims who opposed nationalism altogether. In India, Mawlana Abu'l-A'la' Mawdudi, who was the founder of the Jama'at-i Islami, opposed both secular and religious nationalism and argued for the Islamization of society and an Islamic alternative to nationalism. In Egypt, Sayyid Qutb and Hasan al-Banna', who were the mentors of the Muslim Brotherhood, fought for the educational, moral, and social reform of an Islamic Egypt and indeed of all the Islamic world.

Only a few existing states where Muslims predominate, such as Turkey and Saudi Arabia, had no colonial interval; most became independent after World War II (1939–1945). An even larger number of countries have Muslim minorities. Like the citizens of many new nations, Muslims have not found the creation of national identities to be easy, especially considering the pace at which it has had to occur. More than two-thirds of the world's nations have come into existence since the end of World War II; foreign dependency is a living memory for many of their citizens, or at least for the parents and grandparents of their citizens.

Many Muslim countries are not nation-states—that is, states established by a group of people who decided that they belonged together and therefore went about acquiring sovereignty over a territory—but rather are state-nations, composed of groups of people who acquired or were given sovereignty over a territory and then had to develop a sense of nationality.

The most obvious state-nations are Syria, Iraq, Lebanon, and Jordan. All resulted from the interaction of intra-European rivalry and diplomacy with the aspirations of a prominent Ottoman-Hashimite sharifian family in Mecca to create a single Arab state in the East. Instead of a single state, however, three monarchies emerged: the kingdom of Husayn ibn 'Ali in the Hejaz (to be replaced by the Saudis), the kingdom of Faysal I in

Iraq, and the kingdom of 'Abdullah in Transjordan. Lebanon was carved from French Syria with borders that would establish a bare Christian majority loyal to the French.

In Ottoman Palestine, Jewish nationalists clashed with Arab nationalists at a time when both groups felt betrayed by the British. In subsequent armed clashes, Zionist groups defended a set of boundaries as artificial as many others, creating a state that has remained a target for anti-imperialist sentiment. Eventually, Jewish nationalism spawned another nationalism, that of the Palestinians, inchoate before the founding of Israel but crystallized by the failure of any party to the conflict—Arab states, foreign powers, Palestinian leaders, or Israel itself—to make a place for most of the former Arab residents of Palestine.

Many Muslim countries were united by negative nationalism, aimed at ejecting a common enemy; but turning negative into positive has been difficult. Rarely have the groups that achieved independence survived. Often, as in Libya or Iraq or Egypt, further revolutions have occurred, in many cases led by the military, whose role as a vehicle for modernization cannot be underestimated. Subsequent governments have had to deal with the social and economic problems that plague all developing countries, as well as with regional rivalries and conflicts. Almost nowhere did the colonizers leave an infrastructure sufficient to support the growth of population that European medicine and hygiene had produced.

Given the multicommunal structure of premodern Muslim societies, the relation between religion and nationality has been another major problem. Nationalism has frequently led to competition and rivalry among a new nation's religious communities. As they became independent, citizens of the countries of the Islamic world could draw on no direct equivalent of national identity. The broadest identity was provided by membership in a panterritorial community like the *ummah* of all Muslims or the Greek Orthodox Church or the Turkic tribes; the narrowest, family or neighborhood.

In the middle of the spectrum was membership in a local

confessional community, with all its implications of status, occupation, manners, and customs. Citizens of the new nations would theoretically have to find an identity that could subsume and supersede all others; and the rulers of new nations would have to take the unprecedented step of declaring all citizens subject to the same law, rather than members of quasi-autonomous, self-governing religious communities with their own legal systems. Yet the significance of being a member of a religious community could not easily be undone or replaced.

Many countries inherited a relatively simple form of this problem: the people within their borders were primarily of one faith, Islam, and most were of one form of that faith, the Sunni, except for Iran, which was overwhelmingly Shi'ite, and a small handful of countries with slight Shi'ite majorities. Whatever the predominant sect, that majority adherence could in some way be associated with or bolster the national identity, while discomfiting only a small number of people. Turkey, Iran, Jordan, Indonesia, Yemen, and all the states of North Africa and the Arabian Peninsula fall into this category. Even so, religious minorities in these countries (such as the Armenians) suffered and shrank; for Jews communal lines were hardened by the emergence of the state of Israel, the hostility it evoked from most Arab states, and its aggressive efforts at ingathering. The self-consciously Islamic government in Iran has also introduced a religious intolerance that, while it is discouraged by the Shari'ah, is encouraged by local sentiment as well as by the staunch nationalism Iran shares with secular states. The leaders of the Islamic Republic of Iran have associated being Iranian with being Shi'ite Muslim.

Farther from the center of the Islamic world, Islam plays various roles as a minority religion. Muslims living in Western Europe and the Americas are generally able to form communities and practice their religion as they will: in Canada, for example, Isma'ili Muslims, under the guidance of Aga Khan IV, form a cohesive group that promotes the economic and cultural development of its members. In the United States, tenets of

Islam were embraced by the founders of the American Muslim Mission (originally called Nation of Islam) in the early 1930s. As the community has developed, its leaders have increasingly emphasized the Qur'an and Muhammad's example as sources of authority.

Although Islamic activism never disappeared during the years in which Muslim countries were becoming independent, other ideological orientations seemed more important between the end of World War II and the declaration of the Islamic Republic of Iran in 1979. Many Westerners or Westernized Muslims expected religion to recede as modernization progressed. Already in the 1950s, however, the Muslim Brotherhood in Egypt called for an exclusively Islamic state in place of the secular multicommunal state that Gamal Abdel Nasser had founded. In the early 1960s new circumstances were beginning to foster increased Islamic activity, some popular, some supported by official institutions. In these years critics of Mohammad Reza Shah Pahlavi began to rally around the exiled Ayatollah Ruhollah Khomeini; the writings of 'Ali Shari'ati began to influence Muslims inside and outside Iran; and two great pan-Islamic organizations were formed, the Muslim World League (1962) and the Organization of the Islamic Conference (1971). Although Westerners have become most familiar with activism's violent forms, its educational, cultural, pietistic, and political dimensions have been more extensive. All these developments occurred in the wake of the formation of the OPEC in 1961 and climaxed in Egypt's relatively good showing in its war with Israel in 1973.

The resurgence of economic and military power was not the only factor that could foster those who had maintained an interest in Islam all along. In a few parts of the Muslim world, petroleum-based prosperity promoted increased international influence and pride; elsewhere modernization was producing widespread educational and economic cleavages and populations with very low median ages. In the 1980s and '90s, populations in most Muslim countries soared at the same time economies languished. Even in the oil-rich state of Saudi Arabia, per capita income fell dramatically, and unemployment, for the first time, became a problem. During that time, civil war tormented countries such as Algeria and Lebanon, and in the Persian Gulf, there were three successive wars, two of which—the First and Second Persian Gulf Wars (1990–1991 and 2003)—underscored Muslim military weakness vis-à-vis the West. As dissatisfaction with the material failures of secular modernization grew, so did disenchantment with the Western ideologies that had undergirded it. While these other ideologies were being tried and discredited, Islam had remained relatively peripheral to public policy and thus unassailable. All the while, citizens of Muslim countries were echoing the anti-imperialist rhetoric increasing throughout the developing world. Throughout the Islamic world, Islamic ideas and symbols began to increasingly surface in political dialogue, not just in such revolutionary countries as Iran but also in countries with strong secular traditions such as Turkey. By the early 21st century, almost all political protest movements in the Islamic world were based on a religious orientation. A number of these, radicalized by the Islamic revolution in Iran, brutalized by secular regimes at home, or trained and inspired by military service against the Soviet Union during the Afghan War (1978–1992), sought to overthrow corrupt domestic regimes and undermine the influence of Western countries in the Islamic world.

Judicial System

Iran's 12-member Council of Guardians is a body of jurists—half its members specialists in Islamic canon law appointed by the leader and the other half civil jurists nominated by the Supreme Judicial Council and appointed by the Majles—that acts in many ways as an upper legislative house. The council reviews all legislation passed by the Majles to determine its constitutionality. If a majority of the council does not find a piece of legislation in compliance with the constitution or if a majority of the council's Islamic canon lawyers find the document to be contrary to the standards of Islamic law, then the council may strike it down or return it with revisions to the Majles for reconsideration. In addition, the council supervises elections, and all candidates standing for election—even for the presidency—must meet with its prior approval.

In 1988 Khomeini ordered the formation of the Committee to Determine the Expediency of the Islamic Order—consisting of several members from the Council of Guardians and several members appointed by the president—to arbitrate disagreements between the Majles and the Council of Guardians. The Assembly of Experts, a body of 83 clerics, was originally formed to draft the 1979 constitution. Since that time its sole function has been to select a new leader in the event of the death or incapacitation of the incumbent. If a suitable candidate is not found, the assembly may appoint a governing council of three to five members in the leader's stead.

The judiciary consists of a Supreme Court, a Supreme Judicial Council, and lower courts. The chief justice and the prosecutor general must be specialists in Shi'ite canon law who have attained the status of *mujtahid*. Under the 1979 constitution all judges must base their decisions on the Shari'ah (Islamic law).

In 1982 the Supreme Court struck down any portion of the law codes of the deposed monarchy that did not conform with the Shari'ah. In 1983 the Majles revised the penal code and instituted a system that embraced the form and content of Islamic law. This code implemented a series of traditional punishments, including retributions (Arabic *qisas*) for murder and other violent crimes—wherein the nearest relative of a murdered party may, if the court approves, take the life of the killer.

Violent corporal punishments, including execution, are now the required form of chastisement for a wide range of crimes, ranging from adultery to alcohol consumption. With the number of clergy within the judiciary growing since the revolution, the state in 1987 implemented a special court outside of the regular judiciary to try members of the clergy accused of crimes.

Khamenei, (Ayatollah) Ali

Ayatollah Ali Khamenei.

Born in Mashhad, Iran, on July 15, 1939, Khamenei is an Iranian Shi'ite clergyman and politician who served as president of Iran (1981–1989) and as that country's *rahbar* ("leader") from 1989. A religious figure of some significance, Khamenei is generally addressed with the honorific ayatollah.

Khamenei began his advanced religious studies at Qom under the most prominent Shi'ite scholars of the day, including Ruhollah Khomeini. From 1963 Khamenei was actively involved in protests against the monarchy of Mohammad Reza Shah

Pahlavi, for which he was imprisoned several times by Iran's security services. Khamenei remained closely associated with the exiled Khomeini during this time and immediately after the latter's return to Iran in 1979 was appointed to the Revolutionary Council. After its dissolution he became deputy minister of defense and Khomeini's personal representative on the Supreme Defense Council.

A fiery orator in support of the pro-Khomeini Islamic Republican Party (IRP) and an ardent advocate of the concept of *velayat-e faqih* (governance by the religious jurist), Khamenei was injured in 1981 in one of a series of terrorist bombings that devastated the IRP's upper echelon. Following the death of the secretary-general of the IRP in another such blast later that year, Khamenei was appointed to fill the vacant position and within weeks announced his intention to run for the presidency. He was elected president in October 1981 and reelected in 1985. Although not considered one of Iran's senior clerics— he was then generally accorded the somewhat less lofty title of *hojatoleslam*—Khamenei rose to the position of *rahbar* following the death of Khomeini in 1989. Khamenei enjoyed a good working relationship with President Ali Akbar Hashemi Rafsanjani in the early 1990s, but Khamenei's relations were strained with reformist President Mohammad Khatami, who was elected in 1997.

Khatami, Mohammad

Mohammad Khatami was born in Ardakan, Iran, on September 29, 1943. As the son of a well-known religious teacher, Khatami studied at a traditional *madrasah* in the religious city of Qom (where he later taught). However, he also received degrees in philosophy from Esfahan University and the University of Tehran, both secular institutions, a somewhat unusual accomplishment for a member of Iran's Shi'ite clergy. Khatami held the title *hojatoleslam*, signifying his position as a cleric, and, as a direct descendant of the Prophet Muhammad, he wore a black turban. During the 1960s and '70s Khatami gained a reputation as an opponent of the rule of Mohammad Reza Shah Pahlavi. In 1978 Khatami was appointed head of the Islamic Center in Hamburg, Germany, and after the 1979 Islamic revolution was elected to the Majles, the Iranian national assembly. Khatami held several positions in the Iranian government during the

Mohammad Khatami stands near a Russian oil tanker, 2004.

1980s, including that of minister of culture and Islamic guidance, which he held again in the early 1990s before being forced to resign in 1992 amid allegations that he permitted too much un-Islamic sentiment. He then became the director of the National Library and served as an adviser to President Ali Akbar Hashemi Rafsanjani.

In the 1997 elections Khatami was one of four candidates to run for the presidency and on social issues was the most moderate. With strong support from the country's youth, women, and intellectuals, he was elected by almost 70 percent of the vote. Some of the moderates he appointed to the cabinet were controversial but nonetheless were approved by Iran's conservative Majles. Tension between the president and conservatives grew, however, and, beginning in 1998, a number of key Khatami supporters were prosecuted and harassed as a result. He advocated increased contact with the United States, but his domestic opponents hindered rapprochement between the two countries. Khatami was reelected in 2001 by an overwhelming majority of the vote and served until 2005.

Khomeini, (Ayatollah) Ruhollah

Ruhollah Khomeini was an Iranian Shi'ite cleric who led the revolution that overthrew Mohammad Reza Shah Pahlavi in 1979 and who was Iran's ultimate political and religious authority for the next 10 years.

Little is known of Khomeini's early life. There are various dates given for his birth, the most common being May 17, 1900, and September 24, 1902. He was the grandson and son of mullahs, or Shi'ite religious leaders. When he was five months old, his father was killed on the orders of a local landlord. The young Khomeini was raised by his mother and aunt and then by his older brother. He was educated in various Islamic schools, and he settled in the city of Qom in about 1922. In about 1930 he adopted the name of his hometown, Khomeyn (also spelled Khomein or Khomayn), as his surname. As a Shi'ite scholar and teacher, Khomeini produced numerous writings on Islamic philosophy, law, and ethics, but it was his outspoken opposition to Iran's ruler, Mohammad Reza Shah Pahlavi, his denunciations of Western influences, and his uncompromising advocacy of Islamic purity that won him his initial following in Iran. In the 1950s he was acclaimed as an ayatollah, or major religious leader, and by the early 1960s he had received the title of grand ayatollah, thereby making him one of the supreme religious leaders of the Shi'ite community in Iran.

In 1962–1963 Khomeini spoke out against the shah's reduction of religious estates in a land-reform program and against the emancipation of women. His ensuing arrest sparked antigovernment riots, and, after a year's imprisonment, Khomeini was forcibly exiled from Iran on November 4, 1964. He eventually settled in the Shi'ite holy city of Al-Najaf, Iraq, from where he continued to call for the shah's overthrow and the establishment of an Islamic republic in Iran.

   From the mid-1970s Khomeini's influence inside Iran grew dramatically owing to mounting public dissatisfaction with the shah's regime. Iraq's ruler, Saddam Hussein, forced Khomeini to leave Iraq on October 6, 1978. Khomeini then settled in Neauphle-le-Château, a suburb of Paris. From there his supporters relayed his tape-recorded messages to an increasingly aroused Iranian populace, and massive demonstrations, strikes, and civil unrest in late 1978 forced the departure of the shah from the country on January 16, 1979. Khomeini arrived in Tehran in triumph on February 1, 1979, and was acclaimed as the religious leader of Iran's revolution. He appointed a government four days later and on March 1 again took up residence in Qom. In December a referendum on a new constitution created an Islamic republic in Iran, with Khomeini named Iran's political and religious leader for life.

   Khomeini was able to tap the deep-seated conservatism of the Muslim revolutionaries, who had acquired new vitality by their victory over the shah. Khomeini himself proved unwavering in his determination to transform Iran into a theocratically ruled Islamic state. Iran's Shi'ite clerics largely took over the formulation of governmental policy, while Khomeini arbitrated among the various revolutionary factions and made final decisions on important matters requiring his personal authority. First his regime took political vengeance, with hundreds of people who had worked for the shah's regime reportedly executed. The remaining domestic opposition was then suppressed, its members being systematically imprisoned or killed. According to Khomeini's dictates, Iranian women were required to wear the veil, Western music and alcohol were banned, and the punishments prescribed by Islamic law were reinstated.

   The main thrust of Khomeini's foreign policy was the complete abandonment of the shah's pro-Western orientation and the adoption of an attitude of unrelenting hostility toward both superpowers. In addition, Iran tried to export its brand of

Ayatollah Ruhollah Khomeini greets his supporters, 1979.

Islamic revivalism to neighboring Muslim countries. Khomeini sanctioned Iranian militants' seizure of the U.S. embassy in Tehran (November 4, 1979) and their holding of American diplomatic personnel as hostages for more than a year. He also refused to countenance a peaceful solution to the Iran-Iraq War, which had begun in 1980 and which he insisted on prolonging in the hope of overthrowing Iraq's ruler, Saddam Hussein. Khomeini finally approved a cease-fire in 1988 that effectively ended the war.

Iran's course of economic development foundered under Khomeini's rule, and his pursuit of victory in the Iran-Iraq War ultimately proved futile. But Khomeini was able to retain his charismatic hold over Iran's Shi'ite masses, and he remained the supreme political and religious arbiter in the country until his death in 1989. His gold-domed tomb in Tehran's Behesht-e Zahra' cemetery has since become a shrine for his supporters. Ideologically, he is best remembered for having developed the concept of *velayat-e faqih* (governance by the religious jurist) in a series of lectures and tracts first promulgated during exile in Iraq in the late 1960s and '70s. Khomeini argued therein for the establishment of a theocratic government administered by Islamic jurists in place of corrupt secular regimes. The Iranian constitution of 1979 embodies articles upholding this concept of juristic authority.

Kurds

The Kurds of Iran have been both urban and rural, and they are concentrated in the country's western mountains. This group, which constitutes only a small proportion of Iran's population, has resisted the Iranian government's efforts, both before and after the revolution of 1979, to assimilate them into the mai stream of national life and, along with their fellow Kurds in adjacent regions of Iraq and Turkey, has sought either regional autonomy or the outright establishment of an independent Kurdish state in the region.

The Kurdish language is a West Iranian language related to Persian and Pashto. The Kurds are thought to number from 30 million to 35 million, including major communities in Turkey, Iran, and Iraq and smaller communities in Armenia, Georgia, Kazakhstan, Lebanon, Syria, and various countries of Europe. However, sources for this information differ widely because of differing criteria of ethnicity, religion, and language; statistics may also be manipulated for political purposes.

The traditional Kurdish way of life was nomadic, revolving around sheep and goat herding throughout the Mesopotamian plains and the highlands of Turkey and Iran. Most Kurds practiced only marginal agriculture. The enforcement of national boundaries beginning after World War I (1914–1918) impeded the seasonal migrations of the flocks, forcing most of the Kurds to abandon their traditional ways for village life and settled farming; others entered nontraditional employment.

The prehistory of the Kurds is poorly known, but their ancestors seem to have inhabited the same upland region for millennia. The records of the early empires of Mesopotamia contain frequent references to mountain tribes with names resembling "Kurd." The Kardouchoi whom the Greek historian

Xenophon speaks of in *Anabasis* (they attacked the "Ten Thousand" near modern Zakhu, Iraq, in 401 BC) may have been Kurds, but some scholars dispute this claim. The name Kurd can be dated with certainty to the time of the tribes' conversion to Islam in the seventh century AD. Most Kurds are Sunni Muslims, and among them are many who practice Sufism and other mystical and heretical sects.

Despite their long-standing occupation of a particular region of the world, the Kurds never achieved nation-state status. Their reputation for military prowess has made them much in demand as mercenaries in many armies. The sultan Saladin, best known to the Western world for exploits in the Crusades, epitomizes the Kurdish military reputation.

The principal unit in traditional Kurdish society was the tribe, typically led by a sheikh, or an aga, whose rule was firm. Tribal identification and the sheikh's authority are still felt, though to a lesser degree, in the large urban areas. Detribalization proceeded intermittently as Kurdish culture became urbanized and was nominally assimilated into several countries.

In traditional Kurdish society, marriage was generally endogamous. In nonurban areas, males usually marry at age 20 and females at a significantly younger age. Households typically consist of father, mother, and children. Polygamy, permitted by Islamic law, is sometimes practiced, although it is forbidden by civil law in Turkey. The strength of the extended family's ties to the tribe varies with the way of life. Kurdish women—who traditionally have been more active in public life than Turkish, Arab, and Iranian women—as well as Kurdish men, have taken advantage of urban educational and employment opportunities, especially in prerevolutionary Iran.

Kurdish nationalism, a recent phenomenon, came about through the conjunction of a variety of factors, including British introduction of the concept of private property, the partition of traditional Kurdistan by modern neighboring states, and the influence of British, U.S., and Soviet interests in the Persian Gulf region. These factors and others combined with the flowering of a nationalist movement among a very small minority of urban, intellectual Kurds.

The first Kurdish newspaper, *Kurdistan*, appeared in 1897 and was published at intervals until 1902. It was revived at Istanbul in 1908 (when the first Kurdish political club, with an affiliated cultural society, was also founded) and again in Cairo during World War I (1914–1918). The Treaty of Sèvres, drawn up in 1920, provided for an autonomous Kurdistan but was never ratified; the Treaty of Lausanne (1923), which replaced the Treaty of Sèvres, made no mention of Kurdistan or of the Kurds. Thus the opportunity to unify the Kurds in a nation-state of their own was lost. Indeed, Kurdistan after the war was more fragmented than before, and various separatist movements arose among Kurdish groups.

The Kurds of Turkey received unsympathetic treatment at the hands of the government, which tried to deprive them of their Kurdish identity by designating them "Mountain Turks," by outlawing the Kurdish language (or representing it as a dialect of Turkish), and by forbidding them to wear distinctive Kurdish costumes in or near the important administrative cities. The Turkish government suppressed Kurdish political agitation in the eastern provinces and encouraged the migration of Kurds to the urbanized western portion of Turkey, thus diluting the concentration of Kurdish population in the uplands. Periodic rebellions occurred, and in 1974 a university student, Abdullah Öcalan, formed the Kurdistan Workers Party (known by its Kurdish acronym, PKK), a Marxist organization dedicated to an independent Kurdistan. Operating mainly from eastern Anatolia, PKK fighters engaged in guerrilla operations against government installations and perpetrated frequent acts of terrorism. PKK attacks and government reprisals led to a state of virtual war in eastern Turkey during the 1980s and '90s. Following Öcalan's capture in 1999, PKK activities were sharply curtailed. In 2002, under pressure from the European Union (in which Turkey sought membership), the government legalized broadcasts and education in the Kurdish language.

Kurds also felt strong assimilationist pressure from the national government in Iran and endured religious persecution by that country's Shi'ite Muslim majority. Shortly after World War II (1939–1945), the Soviet Union backed the establishment of an independent country around the largely Kurdish city of Mahabad, in northwestern Iran. The so-called Republic of Mahabad collapsed after Soviet withdrawal in 1947, but about that same time the Kurdish Democratic Party of Iran (KDPI) was established. Thereafter, the KDPI engaged in low-level hostilities with the Iranian government into the 21st century.

Although the pressure for Kurds to assimilate was less intense in Iraq (where the Kurdish language and culture have been freely practiced), government repression has been the most brutal. Short-lived armed rebellions occurred in Iraq in 1931–1932 and 1944–1945, and a low-level armed insurgency took place throughout the 1960s under the command of Mustafa al-Barzani, leader of the Iraqi Kurdish Democratic Party (IKDP), who had been an officer of the Republic of Mahabad. A failed peace accord with the Iraqi government led to another outbreak of fighting in 1975, but an agreement between Iraq and Iran—which had been supporting Kurdish efforts—later that year led to a collapse of Kurdish resistance. Thousands of Kurds fled to Iran and Turkey. Low-intensity fighting followed. In the late 1970s, Iraq's Ba'th Party instituted a policy of settling Iraqi Arabs in parts of Kurdistan— particularly around the oil-rich city of Karkuk—and uprooting Kurds from those same regions. This policy accelerated in the 1980s, as large numbers of Kurds were forcibly relocated, par- ticularly from areas along the Iranian border where Iraqi authorities suspected Kurds were aiding Iranian forces during the Iran-Iraq War (1980–1990). What followed was one of the most brutal episodes in Kurdish history. In a series of operations between March and August 1988, code-named Anfal (Arabic "Spoils"), Iraqi forces sought to quell Kurdish resistance; the Iraqis used large quantities of chemical weapons on Kurdish civilians. In the first attack, on March 16 in and around the village of Halabjah, Iraqi troops killed as many as 5,000 Kurds with mustard gas and nerve agent. Despite these attacks, Kurds again rebelled following Iraq's defeat in the First Persian Gulf War (1990–1991) but were again brutally suppressed—sparking another mass exodus. With the help of the United States, however, the Kurds were able to establish a "safe haven" in most of Iraqi Kurdistan, where the IKDP and Patriotic Union of Kurdistan—a faction that split from the IKDP in 1975—created an autonomous civil authority that was, for the most part, free from interference by the Iraqi government. Kurdish fighters again supported U.S. and allied forces when they overthrew the Ba'th regime during the Second Persian Gulf War (2003).

Land

Iran occupies a high plateau rising over 1,500 feet above sea level and is surrounded largely by mountains. In the north rise the towering Elburz Mountains, which run along the southern shore of the Caspian Sea and reach heights above 17,000 feet. Iran's largest mountain range, the Zagros, stretches along the southwestern side of the country. More than half of the country's surface area consists of salt deserts and other wasteland. Streams are seasonal, and much of Iran's interior drainage flows

Pastures along the Zagros Mountains.

into saline marshes. The Karun River, in the west, is the c̶try's only navigable stream. About one-tenth of its land is arable, another one-fourth is suitable for grazing, and some one-eighth is forested, mostly near the Caspian Sea. Iran's rich petroleum deposits account for about one-tenth of world reserves, and its natural-gas deposits constitute about one-seventh of the world total; they are the basis of the country's economy.

ıad Reza Shah

Mohammad Reza Shah Pahlavi, 1979.

Mohammad Reza Shah Pahlavi (1919–1980) was the shah of Iran from 1941 to 1979. He maintained a pro-Western foreign policy and fostered economic development in Iran.

Mohammad Reza was the eldest son of Reza Shah Pahlavi, an army officer who became the ruler of Iran and founder of the Pahlavi dynasty in 1925. Mohammad Reza was educated in Switzerland and returned to Iran in 1935. In 1941 the Soviet Union and Great Britain, fearing that the shah would cooperate with Nazi Germany to rid himself of their tutelage, occupied Iran and forced Reza Shah into exile. Mohammad Reza then replaced his father on the throne (September 16, 1941).

In the early 1950s a struggle for control of the Iranian government developed between the shah and Mohammad

Mosaddeq, a zealous Iranian nationalist. In March 1951 Mosaddeq secured passage of a bill in the Majles (parliament) to nationalize the vast British petroleum interests in Iran. Mosaddeq's power grew rapidly, and by the end of April Mohammad Reza had been virtually forced to appoint Mosaddeq premier. A two-year period of tension and conflict followed. In August 1953 the shah tried to dismiss Mosaddeq but was himself forced to leave the country by Mosaddeq's supporters. Several days later, however, Mosaddeq's opponents, with the covert support and assistance of the United States and Britain, restored Mohammad Reza to power.

The shah reversed Mosaddeq's nationalization. With U.S. assistance the shah then carried out a national development program, called the White Revolution, that included construction of an expanded road, rail, and air network, a number of dam and irrigation projects, the eradication of diseases such as malaria, the encouragement and support of industrial growth, and land reform. He also established a literacy corps and a health corps for the large but isolated rural population. In the 1960s and '70s Mohammad Reza sought to develop a more independent foreign policy and established working relationships with the Soviet Union and Eastern European nations.

The White Revolution solidified domestic support for the monarch, but he faced continuing political criticism from those who felt that the reforms did not move far or fast enough, and religious criticism from those who believed Westernization to be antithetical to the Islamic character of the country. Opposition to the shah was based upon his autocratic rule, corruption in his government, the unequal distribution of oil wealth, forced Westernization, and the activities of SAVAK (the secret police) in suppressing dissent and opposition to his rule. These negative aspects of Mohammad Reza's rule became markedly accentuated after Iran began to reap greater revenues from its petroleum exports beginning in 1973. Widespread dissatisfaction among the lower classes, the Shi'ite clergy, the bazaar merchants, and students led in 1978 to the growth of support for the Ayatollah Ruhollah Khomeini, a Shi'ite religious leader living in exile near Paris. Rioting and turmoil in Iran's major cities brought down four successive governments; on January 16, 1979, the Iranian monarch, beleaguered by opponents and weakened by cancer, left the country, and Khomeini assumed control. Although the shah did not abdicate, a referendum resulted in the declaration on April 1, 1979, of an Islamic republic in Iran. The shah traveled to Egypt, Morocco, the Bahamas, and Mexico before entering the United States on October 22, 1979, for medical treatment of lymphatic cancer. Two weeks later Iranian militants seized the U.S. embassy in Tehran and took hostage 66 American citizens, demanding the extradition of Mohammad Reza in return for the hostages' release. Extradition was refused, but the shah later left for Panama and then Cairo, where he was granted asylum by President Anwar el-Sadat.

The shah had three marriages, two of which ended in divorce when they failed to produce a male heir to the throne. Of Mohammad Reza's numerous siblings, he was especially close to his twin sister, Ashraf, a forceful woman who had a powerful influence on the monarch but with whom he is said to have had a sometimes turbulent relationship.

Mosaddeq, Mohammad

Mohammad Mosaddeq.

Born in Tehran, Iran, in 1880, Mosaddeq was the son of an Iranian public official and grew up as a member of Iran's ruling elite. He received a doctor of law degree from the University of Lausanne in Switzerland and then returned to Iran in 1914 and was appointed governor-general of the important Fars Province. He remained in the government following the rise to power of Reza Khan in 1921 and served as minister of finance and then briefly as minister of foreign affairs. Mosaddeq was elected to the Majles (parliament) in 1923. When the Majles named Reza Khan shah in 1925, however, Mosaddeq opposed the move and was compelled to retire to private life.

Mosaddeq reentered public service in 1944, following Reza Shah's forced abdication in 1941, and was elected again to the

Majles. An outspoken advocate of nationalism, he soon played a leading part in successfully opposing the grant to the Soviet Union of an oil concession for northern Iran similar to an existing British concession in southern Iran. He built considerable political strength, based largely on his call to nationalize the concession as well as the installations of the British-owned Anglo-Iranian Oil Company located in Iran. In March 1951 the Majles passed his oil nationalization act, and his power had grown so great that the shah, Mohammad Reza Pahlavi, was virtually forced to appoint him premier.

The nationalization resulted in a deepening crisis in Iran, both politically and economically. Mosaddeq and his National Front Party continued to gain power but alienated many supporters, particularly among the ruling elite and among Western countries with vested interests in Iran. The British soon withdrew completely from the Iranian oil market, and economic problems increased when Mosaddeq could not readily find alternate markets for Iranian oil.

A continuing struggle for control of the Iranian government developed between Mosaddeq and the shah. In August 1953, when the shah attempted to dismiss the premier, mobs of Mosaddeq followers took to the streets and forced the shah to leave the country. Within a few days, however, Mosaddeq's opponents, with U.S. support, overthrew his government and restored the shah to power. Mosaddeq was sentenced to three years' imprisonment for treason and, after he had served his sentence, was kept under house arrest for the rest of his life, which ended March 5, 1967. The Iranian oil-production facilities remained under control of the Iranian government.

Mosaddeq's personal behavior, which included wearing pajamas for numerous public appearances, speeches to the Majles from his bed (which was brought into the chambers), and frequent bouts of public weeping, helped focus world attention upon him during his premiership. Supporters claim the behavior was a result of illness; detractors say he had a shrewd sense of public relations.

Oil

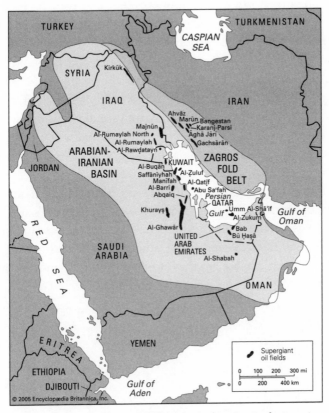

Major oil fields of the Arabian-Iranian basin region.

As home to much of the world's proven oil and natural gas reserves, the Middle East plays a vital role in the global economy. The Arabian-Iranian sedimentary basin sits atop some two-thirds of the world's several dozen "supergiant" oil fields (defined as containing more than 5 billion barrels of ultimately recoverable oil). Iran itself contains about 125 billion barrels of proven oil reserves—roughly one-tenth of the world total. As a result, the extraction and processing of petroleum are unquestionably Iran's most important economic activities and the most valuable in terms of revenue, although natural-gas production also is increasingly important. Oil exports account for about four-fifths of Iran's total export earnings and provide revenue for some two-fifths to half of the government's budget. The government-operated National Iranian Oil Company (NIOC) produces petroleum for export and domestic consumption. Petroleum is moved by pipeline to the terminal of Khark (Kharq) Island in the Persian Gulf and from there is shipped by tanker throughout the world. Iran's main refining facility at Abadan was destroyed during the war with Iraq, but the government has since rebuilt the facility, and production has returned to near prewar levels.

Iran's vast natural gas reserves constitute more than one-tenth of the world's total. In addition to the country's working gas fields in the Elburz Mountains and in Khorasan, fields have been discovered and exploitation begun in the Persian Gulf near 'Asaluyeh; offshore in the Caspian region; and, most notably,

Oil pipeline near Masjed-e Soleyman.

offshore and onshore in areas of southern Iran—the South Pars field in the latter region is one of the richest in the world. The two state-owned Iranian Gas Trunk Lines are the largest gas pipelines in the Middle East, and Iran is under contract to supply natural gas to Russia, Eastern Europe, Pakistan, Turkey, and India through pipelines, under construction in neighboring countries, that are intended to connect Iran's trunk lines with those of its customers.

The petrochemical industry, concentrated in the south of the country, expanded rapidly before the Islamic revolution. It, too, was largely destroyed during the Iran-Iraq War but has mostly been restored to its prewar condition.

Iran's oil industry was established at the turn of the 20th century. In 1901 William Knox D'Arcy, an Englishman businessman who had become wealthy through gold mining in Australia, sent a representative to Tehran to enter into negotiations, and on May 28, 1901, D'Arcy was given a 60-year oil concession. By 1908 D'Arcy's operations had discovered a large oil field in southwest Iran, and the following year the Anglo-Persian Oil Company (later the Anglo-Iranian Oil Company and now British Petroleum) was incorporated. The extensive oil field was soon connected by a 135-mile-long pipeline with a refinery on Abadan Island, and in 1914 the British government became the Anglo-Persian Oil Company's principal stockholder. Other Iranian fields and refineries were built, and by 1938 Abadan had the single largest refinery in the world. D'Arcy's concession was revised in 1933, and from 1951 to 1953, when Mohammad Mosaddeq's government nationalized Britain's oil holdings, the concession was suspended. In 1953 an international consortium was formed between Dutch and U.S. oil companies and the Anglo-Iranian Oil Company. The following year the consortium opened negotiations with the Iranian government and the NIOC (which had been formed to take over the assets and installations of the Anglo-Iranian Oil Company when it was nationalized). In September 1954 an agreement was reached that enabled the resumption of oil activities by two operating companies; the 25-year agreement provided the Iranian government with half of the profits of the oil exported.

In 1960 Iran became a founding member of the Organization of the Petroleum Exporting Countries (OPEC), which was formed to coordinate the petroleum policies of its members. OPEC members, which include African and Latin American countries, collectively own two-thirds of the world's proven petroleum reserves and account for two-fifths of its oil production. Four OPEC members—Kuwait, Qatar, Saudi Arabia, and the United Arab Emirates—have very large per capita oil reserves; they also are relatively strong financially and thus have considerable flexibility in adjusting their production. Saudi Arabia, which has the largest reserves and a relatively small (but fast-growing) population, has traditionally played a dominant role in determining overall production and prices. OPEC often has been beset by internal conflicts, and some experts have concluded that it has not been an effective cartel and has little if any influence over the amount of oil produced or its price. Other experts believe that OPEC has been an effective cartel, though it has not been equally effective at all times. Such experts who claim that OPEC is indeed a cartel and an effective one argue that production costs in the Persian Gulf are generally less than 10 percent of the price charged and that prices would decline toward those costs in the absence of coordination by OPEC.

The influence of individual OPEC members on the organization and on the oil market usually depends on their levels of reserves and production. Saudi Arabia, which controls the largest share of OPEC's total oil reserves, plays a leading role. Iran, Iraq, Kuwait, and the United Arab Emirates, whose combined reserves are significantly greater than those of Saudi Arabia, are also key players. Kuwait, which has a very small population, has shown a willingness to cut production relative to the size of its reserves, whereas Iran and Iraq, both with large and growing populations, have generally produced at high levels relative to reserves. Revolutions and wars have impaired the ability of some OPEC members to maintain high levels of production.

When OPEC was formed, its main goal was to prevent its concessionaires—the world's largest oil producers, refiners, and marketers—from lowering the price of oil, which they had always specified, or "posted." OPEC members sought to gain greater control over oil prices by coordinating their production and export policies, though each member retained ultimate control over its own policy. OPEC managed to prevent price reductions during the 1960s, but its success encouraged increases in production, resulting in a gradual decline in nominal prices (not adjusted for inflation) from $1.93 per barrel in 1955 to $1.30 per barrel in 1970. During the 1970s the primary goal of OPEC members was to secure complete sovereignty over their petroleum resources. Accordingly, several OPEC members nationalized their oil reserves and altered their contracts with major oil companies.

In October 1973 OPEC raised oil prices by 70 percent. In December, two months after the Yom Kippur War, prices were raised by an additional 130 percent, and the organization's Arab members (which did not include Iran, an ethnically Persian country), which had formed OAPEC (Organization of Arab Petroleum Exporting Countries) in 1968, curtailed production and placed an embargo on oil shipments to the United States and the Netherlands, the main supporters of Israel during the war. The result throughout the West was severe oil shortages and spiraling inflation. As OPEC continued to raise prices through the rest of the decade (prices increased tenfold from 1973 to 1980), its political and economic power grew.

Although oil-importing countries reacted slowly to the price increases, eventually they reduced their overall energy consumption, found other sources of oil (e.g., in Norway, the United Kingdom, and Mexico), and developed alternative sources of energy such as coal, natural gas, and nuclear power. In response, OPEC members—particularly Saudi Arabia and Kuwait—reduced their production levels in the early 1980s in what proved to be a futile effort to defend their posted prices. Production and prices continued to fall in the 1980s. Although the brunt of the production cuts were borne by Saudi Arabia, whose oil revenues shrank by some four-fifths by 1986, the revenues of all producers, including non-OPEC countries, fell by some two-thirds in the same period as the price of oil dropped to less than $10 per barrel. The decline in revenues and the ruinous Iran-Iraq War (1980–1990) undermined the unity of the organization and precipitated a major policy shift by Saudi Arabia, which decided that it no longer would defend the price of oil but would defend its market share instead. Following Saudi Arabia's lead, other OPEC members soon decided to maintain production quotas. Saudi Arabia's influence within OPEC also was evident during the First Persian Gulf War (1990–1991)—which resulted from the invasion of one OPEC member (Kuwait) by another (Iraq)—when the kingdom agreed to increase production to stabilize prices and minimize any disruption in the international oil market.

During the 1990s OPEC continued to emphasize production quotas. Oil prices, which collapsed at the end of the decade, began to increase again in the early 21st century (dramatically so from 2004), owing to greater unity among OPEC members and better cooperation with nonmembers (such as Mexico, Norway, Oman, and Russia), increased tensions in the Middle East, a political crisis in Venezuela, and growing consumption in new markets.

People

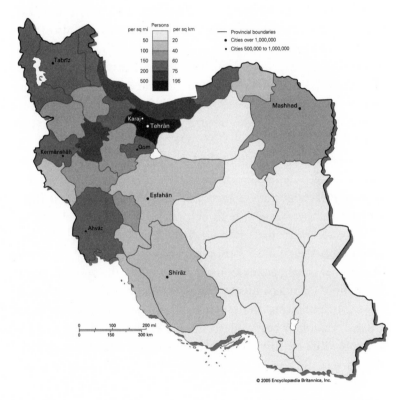

per sq mi | Persons | per sq km
50 | | 20
100 | | 40
150 | | 60
200 | | 75
500 | | 195

—— Provincial boundaries
● Cities over 1,000,000
● Cities 500,000 to 1,000,000

Tabriz

Mashhad

Karaj ● Tehrān

Kermānshāh

Qom

Eṣfahān

Ahvāz

Shīrāz

0   100   200 mi
0   150   300 km

© 2005 Encyclopædia Britannica, Inc.

Population density in Iraq.

Ethnic Groups

Iran is a culturally diverse society, and interethnic relations are generally amicable. The predominant ethnic and cultural group in the country consists of native speakers of Persian. But the people who are generally known as Persians are of mixed ancestry, and the country has important Turkic and Arab elements in addition to the Kurds, Balochi, Bakhtyari, Lurs, and other smaller minorities (Armenians, Assyrians, Jews, Brahuis, and others). The Persians, Kurds, and speakers of other Indo-European languages in Iran are descendants of the Aryan tribes that began migrating from Central Asia into what is now Iran in the second millennium BC. Those of Turkic ancestry are the progeny of tribes that appeared in the region—also from Central Asia—beginning in the 11th century AD, and the Arab minority settled predominantly in the country's southwest (in Khuzestan, a region also known as Arabistan) following the Islamic conquests of the seventh century. Like the Persians, many of Iran's smaller ethnic groups chart their arrival into the region to ancient times.

The Kurds have traditionally been a nomadic people dwelling in the western mountains of Iran. This group, which constitutes only a small proportion of Iran's population, has resisted the Iranian government's efforts, both before and after the revolution of 1979, to assimilate them into the mainstream of national life and, along with their fellow Kurds in adjacent regions of Iraq and Turkey, has sought either regional autonomy or the outright establishment of an independent Kurdish state in the region.

Also inhabiting the western mountains are seminomadic Lurs, thought to be the descendants of the aboriginal inhabitants of the country. Closely related are the Bakhtyari tribes, who live in the Zagros Mountains west of Esfahan. The Balochi are a smaller minority who inhabit Iranian Baluchistan, which borders on Pakistan.

The largest Turkic group is the Azerbaijanians, a farming and herding people who inhabit two border provinces in the northwestern corner of Iran. Two other Turkic ethnic groups are the Qashqa'i, in the Shiraz area to the north of the Persian Gulf, and the Turkmen, of Khroasan in the northeast.

The Armenians, with a different ethnic heritage, are concentrated in Tehran, Esfahan, and the Azerbaijan region and are engaged primarily in commercial pursuits. A few isolated groups speaking Dravidian dialects are found in the Sistan region to the southeast.

Semites—Jews, Assyrians, and Arabs—constitute only a small percentage of the population. The Jews trace their heritage in Iran to the Babylonian Exile of the sixth century and, like the Armenians, have retained their ethnic, linguistic, and religious identity. Both groups traditionally have clustered in the largest cities. The Assyrians are concentrated in the northwest, and the Arabs live in Khuzestan as well as on the Persian Gulf islands.

Religion

The vast majority of Iranians are Muslims of the Ithna 'Ashari, or Twelver, Shi'ite branch, which is the official state religion. The Kurds and Turkmen are predominantly Sunni Muslims, but Iran's Arabs are both Sunni and Shi'ite. Small communities of Christians, Jews, and Zoroastrians are also found throughout the country.

The two cornerstones of Iranian Shi'ism are the promise of the return of the divinely inspired 12th imam—Muhammad al-Mahdi al-Hujjah, whom Shi'ites believe to be the mahdi—and the veneration of his martyred forebears. The absence of the imam contributed indirectly to the development in modern Iran of a strong Shi'ite clergy whose penchant for status, particularly in the 20th century, led to a proliferation of titles and honorifics unique in the Islamic world. The Shi'ite clergy have been the predominant political and social force in Iran since the 1979 revolution.

Those progeny of the family of Muhammad who are not his direct descendents through the line of the 12th imam are referred to as sayyids. These individuals have traditionally been viewed with a high degree of reverence by believing Iranians and continue to have strong influence in contemporary Iranian culture. Many sayyids are found among the clergy, although in modern Iran they may practice virtually any occupation.

Christians, Jews, and Zoroastrians are the most significant religious minorities. Christians are the most numerous group of these, Orthodox Armenians constituting the bulk. The Assyrians are Nestorian, Protestant, and Roman Catholic, as are a few converts from other ethnic groups. The Zoroastrians are largely concentrated in Yazd in central Iran, Kerman in the southeast, and Tehran.

Religious toleration, one of the characteristics of Iran during the Pahlavi monarchy, came to an end with the Islamic revolution in 1979. While Christians, Jews, and Zoroastrians are recognized in the constitution of 1979 as official minorities, the revolutionary atmosphere in Iran was not conducive to equal treatment of non-Muslims. Among these, members of the Baha'i faith—a religion founded in Iran—were the victims of the greatest persecution. The Jewish population, which had been significant before 1979, emigrated in great numbers after the revolution.

Settlement Patterns

Rural Settlement

The topography and the water supply determine the regions fit for human habitation, the lifestyles of the people, and the types of dwellings. The deep gorges and defiles, unnavigable rivers, empty deserts, and impenetrable *kavirs* (salt deserts) have all contributed to insularity and tribalism among the Iranian peoples, and the population has become concentrated around the periphery of the interior plateau and in the oases. The felt yurts of the Turkmen, the black tents of the Bakhtyari, and the osier huts of the Balochi are typical, as the tribespeople roam from summer to winter pastures. The vast central and southern plains are dotted with numerous oasis settlements with scattered rudimentary hemispherical or conical huts. Since the mid-20th century the migrations have shortened, and the nomads have settled in more permanent villages.

The villages on the plains follow an ancient rectangular pattern. High mud walls with corner towers form the outer face of the houses, which have flat roofs of mud and straw supported by wooden rafters. A mosque is situated in the open center of the village and serves also as a school.

Mountain villages are situated on the rocky slopes above the valley floor, surrounded by terraced fields (usually irrigated) in which grain and alfalfa (lucerne) are raised. The houses are square, mud-brick, windowless buildings with flat or domed roofs; a roof hole provides ventilation and light. Houses are usually two stories high, with a stable occupying the ground floor.

Caspian villages are different from those of both the plains and the mountains. The scattered hamlets typically consist of two-storied wooden houses. Separate outbuildings (barns, hen-houses, silkworm houses) surround an open courtyard.

Urban Settlement

Tehran, the capital and largest city, is separated from the Caspian Sea by the Elburz Mountains. Esfahan, about 250 miles south of Tehran, is the second most important city and is famed for its architecture. There are few cities in central and eastern Iran, where water is scarce, although lines of oases penetrate the desert. Most towns are supplied with water by *qanat*, an irrigation system by which an underground mountain water source is tapped and the water channeled down through a series of tunnels, sometimes 50 miles in length, to the town level. Therefore, towns are often located a short distance from the foot of a mountain. The essential feature of a traditional Iranian street is a small canal.

City layout is typical of Islamic communities. The various sectors of society—governmental, residential, and business—are often divided into separate quarters. The business quarter, or bazaar, fronting on a central square, is a maze of narrow arcades lined with small individual shops grouped according to the type of product sold. Modern business centers, however, have grown up outside the bazaars. Dwellings in the traditional style—consisting of domed-roof structures constructed of mud brick or stone—are built around closed courtyards, with a garden and a pool. Public baths are found in all sections of the cities.

Construction of broad avenues and ring roads to accommodate modern traffic has changed the appearance of the large cities. Their basic plan, however, is still that of a labyrinth of narrow, crooked streets and culs-de-sac.

Demographic Trends

Iran is a young country: nearly two-fifths of its people are 15 years of age or younger. However, the country's postrevolutionary boom in births has slowed substantially, and—with a birth rate slightly lower than the world average and a low death rate—Iran's natural rate of increase is now only marginally higher than the world average. Life expectancy in Iran is some 68 years for men and 71 years for women.

Internal migration from rural areas to cities was a major trend beginning in the 1960s (some three-fifths of Iranians are defined as urban), but the most significant demographic phenomenon following the revolution in 1979 was the outmigration of a large portion of the educated, secularized population to Western countries, particularly to the United States. (Several hundred thousand Iranians had settled in Southern California alone by the end of the 20th century.) Likewise, a considerable number of religious minorities, mostly Jews and Baha'is, have left the country—either as emigrants or asylum seekers—because of unfavorable political conditions. Internally, migration to the cities has continued, and Iran has absorbed large numbers of refugees from neighboring Afghanistan (mostly Persian [Dari]-speaking Afghans) and Iraq (both Arabs and Kurds).

Persia

Persia is the historic region of southwestern Asia that is only roughly coterminous with modern Iran. The term Persia was used for centuries, chiefly in the West, to designate those regions where Persian language and culture predominated, but it more correctly refers to a region of southern Iran formerly known as Persis, alternatively as Pars or Parsa, modern Fars. Parsa was the name of an Indo-European nomadic people who migrated into the region in about 1000 BC. The first mention of Parsa occurs in the annals of Shalmanesar II, an Assyrian king, in 844 BC.

During the rule of the Persian Achaemenian dynasty (559–330 BC), the ancient Greeks first encountered the inhabitants of Persis on the Iranian plateau, when the Achaemenids—natives of Persis—were expanding their political sphere. The Achaemenids were the dominant dynasty during Greek history until the time of Alexander the Great, and use of the name Persia was gradually extended by the Greeks and other peoples to apply to the whole Iranian plateau. This tendency was reinforced with the rise of the Sasanian dynasty, also native to Persis, whose culture dominated the Iranian plateau until the seventh century AD. The people of this area have traditionally referred to the region as Iran, "Land of the Aryans," and in 1935 the government of Iran requested that the name Iran be used in lieu of Persia.

The two terms, however, are often used interchangeably when referring to periods preceding the 20th century.

Political System

Iran's 1979 constitution established the country as an Islamic republic and put into place a mixed system of government, in which the executive, parliament, and judiciary are overseen by several bodies dominated by the clergy. At the head of both the state and oversight institutions is the leader, or *rahbar*, a ranking cleric whose duties and authority are those usually equated with a head of state.

The justification for Iran's mixed system of government can be found in the concept of *velayat-e faqih* as expounded by Ayatollah Ruhollah Khomeini, the first leader of postrevolutionary Iran. Khomeini's method gives political leadership—in the absence of the divinely inspired imam—to the *faqih*, or jurist in Islamic canon law, whose characteristics best qualify him to lead the community. Khomeini, the leader of the revolution, was widely believed to be such a man, and through his authority the position of leader was enshrined in the Iranian constitution. The Assembly of Experts (Majles-e Khobregan), an institution composed of *'ulama'*, chooses the leader from among qualified Shi'ite clergy on the basis of the candidate's personal piety, expertise in Islamic law, and political acumen. The powers of the leader are extensive; he appoints the senior officers of the military and Revolutionary Guards, as well as the clerical members of the Council of Guardians and members of the judiciary. The leader is also exclusively responsible for declarations of war and is the commander in chief of Iran's armed forces. Most important, the leader sets the general direction of the nation's policy. There are no limits on the leader's term in office, but the Assembly of Experts may remove the leader from office if they find that he is unable to execute his duties.

Upon the death of Khomeini in June 1989, the Assembly of Experts elected Ayatollah Ali Khamenei as his successor, an unexpected move because of Khamenei's relatively low clerical status at the time of his nomination as leader. He was eventually accepted by Iranians as an ayatollah, however, through the urging of senior clerics—a unique event in Shi'ite Islam—and was elevated to the position of *rahbar* because of his political acumen.

The president, who is elected by universal adult suffrage, heads the executive branch and must be a native-born Iranian Shi'ite. This post was largely ceremonial until July 1989, when a national referendum approved a constitutional amendment that abolished the post of prime minister and vested greater authority in the president. The president selects the Council of Ministers for approval by the legislature; appoints a portion of the members of the Committee to Determine the Expediency of the Islamic Order; and serves as chairman of the Supreme Council for National Security, which oversees the country's defense. The president and his ministers are responsible for the day-to-day administration of the government and the implementation of laws enacted by the legislature. In addition, the president oversees a wide range of government offices and organizations.

The unicameral legislature is the 290-member Islamic Consultative Assembly, known simply as the Majles. Deputies are elected directly for four-year terms by universal adult suffrage, and recognized religious and ethnic minorities have token representation in the legislature. The Majles enacts all legislation and, under extraordinary circumstances, may impeach the president with a two-thirds majority vote.

Under the constitution, elections are to be held at least every four years, supervised by the Council of Guardians. Suffrage is universal, and the minimum voting age is 16. All important matters are subject to referenda. At the outset of the revolution, the Islamic Republic Party was the ruling political party in Iran, but it subsequently proved to be too volatile, and Khomeini ordered it disbanded in 1987. The Muslim People's

Republic Party, which once claimed more than 3 million members, and its leader, Ayatollah Mohammad Kazem Shariat-Madari, opposed many of Khomeini's reforms and the ruling party's tactics in the early period of the Islamic republic, but in 1981 it, too, was ordered to dissolve.

The government has likewise outlawed several parties—including the Tudeh ("Masses") Party, the Mojahedin-e Khalq ("Holy Warriors for the People") Party, and the Democratic Party of Iranian Kurdistan—although it permits parties that demonstrate what it considers to be a "commitment to the Islamic system."

Rafsanjani, Ali Akbar Hashemi

Born in 1934, the Iranian politician Ali Akbar Hashemi Rafsanjani is the son of a prosperous farmer in the town of Rafsanjan, in the Kerman region of Iran. He moved to the Shi'ite holy city of Qom in 1948 to pursue his religious studies, and in 1958 he became a disciple of Ruhollah Khomeini. Rafsanjani became a *hojatoleslam* (from the Arabic *hujjat al-islam*, "proof of Islam"), the second-highest Shi'ite Muslim rank (after that of ayatollah). Like Khomeini, he opposed Mohammad Reza Shah Pahlavi's modernization program, and when Khomeini was exiled from Iran in 1962, Rafsanjani became his chief fund-raiser inside the country. Rafsanjani spent the years 1975–1978 in jail in Iran on charges of links with left-wing terrorists.

With the shah's overthrow and Khomeini's return to Iran in 1979, Rafsanjani became one of Khomeini's chief lieutenants. Rafsanjani helped found the Islamic Republican Party, served on the Revolutionary Council, and was acting interior minister during the early years of the revolution. He was also elected to the Majlis (parliament) in 1980, and he became that body's Speaker the same year.

As the dominant voice in the Majlis for the next nine years, Rafsanjani gradually emerged as the second most powerful figure in Iran's government. He was intimately involved in Iran's prosecution of the Iran-Iraq War (1980–1990), and he helped persuade Khomeini to agree to the cease-fire of August 1988 that effectively ended the war.

After Khomeini's death in June 1989, Rafsanjani was elected Iran's president by an overwhelming margin in July. He quickly garnered increased powers for a previously weak executive office, and he showed considerable political skill in promoting his pragmatic policies in the face of resistance from Islamic hard-liners. Rafsanjani favored reducing Iran's international isolation and renewing its ties with Europe as part of a strategy to use foreign investment and free enterprise to revive the country's war-torn economy. Rafsanjani left the presidency in 1997 and occupied several government offices in subsequent years.

Reforms

The Iran-Iraq War cease-fire of 1988 redirected attention to long-standing factional conflicts over economic, social, and foreign policy objectives that had arisen among several groups in Iran's government. "Conservatives" favored less government control of the economy, while "leftists" sought greater economic socialization. These two blocs, both committed to social and religious conservatism, were increasingly challenged by a "pragmatist" or "reformist" bloc. The latter favored steps to normalize relations with the West, ease strict social restrictions, and open up the country's political system as the only solution to their country's crushing economic and social problems, deeply exacerbated by eight years of war.

Change began in short order, when the Assembly of Experts appointed President Ali Khamenei *rahbar* following the death of Ruhollah Khomeini in June 1989. The following month elections were held to select Khamenei's replacement as president. Running virtually unopposed, Hojatoleslam Ali Akbar Hashemi Rafsanjani, Speaker of the Majles since 1980, was elected by an overwhelming vote. Rafsanjani, whose cabinet choices represented the various factions, immediately began the process of rebuilding the war-torn economy. Considered a pragmatist and one of the most powerful men in Iran, Rafsanjani favored a policy of economic liberalization, privatization of industry, and rapprochement with the West that would encourage much-needed foreign investment. The new president's policies were opposed by both Khamenei and the conservative parliament, and attempts by conservative elements to stifle reforms by harassing and imprisoning political dissidents frequently resulted in demonstrations and violent protests, which were often brutally suppressed.

In this new political atmosphere, advocates of women's rights joined with filmmakers who continued to address the gender inequities of the Islamic republic. New forms of communication, including satellite dishes and the Internet, created for Iranians access to Western media and exile groups abroad, who in turn helped broadcast dissident voices from within Iran. International campaigns for human rights, women's rights, and a nascent democratic civil society in Iran began to take root.

President Rafsanjani pushed for restoring economic relations with the West, but, despite its long conflict with Iraq, Iran chose not to join the United Nations multinational force opposing the invasion of Kuwait. In autumn 1991 Iran moved toward reducing its involvement in Lebanon, which facilitated the release of Westerners held hostage there by Lebanese Shi'ite extremists. However, the Iranian government opposed the Israeli-Palestinian peace process and continued to support Islamic groups in Lebanon and in areas under the control of the newly created Palestinian Authority. Iran also allegedly gave financial support to Islamic activists, both Sunni and Shi'ite, in Algeria, Sudan, Afghanistan, and Tajikistan.

Relations with Western Europe and the United States fluctuated. The bounty placed by Iran's government on Anglo-Indian author Salman Rushdie on charges of blasphemy, as well as the state-supported assassinations of dozens of prominent Iranian dissidents in Europe, prevented Iran from normalizing relations with many Western European countries. In 1992 Sadeqh Sharafkandi, a prominent member of the Democratic Party of Iranian Kurdistan, and three of his aides were gunned down in Berlin. The case against those held responsible for the attack was tried in German courts for four years, and in 1997 German authorities indirectly implicated Iranian leaders, including both President Rafsanjani and Ayatollah Khamenei, in the killings. Germany cut off diplomatic and trade relations with Iran, but other European governments continued their economic ties, preventing Iran's complete isolation.

Most Iranian dissident groups in exile gradually shed their

divergent views and agreed that they should work for a democratic political order in Iran. One remaining exception was the National Liberation Army of Iran, a leftist Islamic group based in Iraq that was set up by the Mojahedin-e Khalq. But change was evident even in this organization; its officer corps had become mostly female, including many educated Iranians from Europe and the United States.

Inside Iran in the mid-1990s, Abdolkarim Soroush, a philosopher with training in both secular and religious studies, attracted thousands of followers to his lectures. Soroush advocated a type of reformist Islam that went beyond most liberal Muslim thinkers of the 20th century and argued that the search for reconciliation of Islam and democracy was not a matter of simply finding appropriate phrases in the Qur'an that were in agreement with modern science, democracy, or human rights. Drawing on the works of Immanuel Kant, G. W. F. Hegel, Karl Popper, and Erich Fromm, Soroush called for a reexamination of all tenets of Islam, insisting on the need to maintain the religion's original spirit of social justice and its emphasis on caring for other people.

The May 1997 election of Mohammad Khatami, a supporter of Soroush, as president was a surprise for conservatives who had backed Ali Akbar Nateq-Nouri, Speaker of Iran's Majles. Shortly before the elections, the Council of Guardians had placed Khatami on the list of four acceptable candidates in order to give a greater semblance of democracy to the process. Khatami had been Iran's minister of culture and Islamic guidance but was forced to resign in 1992 for having adopted a more moderate view on social and cultural issues. The new president, who campaigned on a platform of curbing censorship, fighting religious excess, and allowing for greater tolerance, was embraced by much of the public, receiving more than two-thirds of the vote and enjoying especially strong support among women and young adults.

The election of Khatami, and his appointment of a more moderate cabinet, unleashed a wave of euphoria among reformers. In less than a year some 900 new newspapers and journals received authorization to publish and added their voices to earlier reformist journals such as *Zanan* and *Kiyan*, which had been the strongest backers of Khatami. However, the limits of the reformist president's authority became clear in the months after his election. Iran's leader, Ayatollah Khamenei, continued to exercise sweeping executive powers, which he did not hesitate to use to thwart Khatami's reforms. In June 1998 the parliament removed Khatami's liberal interior minister, Abdullah Nouri, in a vote of no confidence, and Tehran's mayor, Gholamhussein Karbaschi, was convicted of corruption and jailed by the president's conservative opponents despite strong public opinion in his favor. Reformist newspapers one by one were accused of offending Islamic principles and shut down, and six prominent intellectuals, including secular nationalist leader Dariyush Farouhar and his wife, Parvaneh Eskandari, were assassinated. Their murders were traced to agents of the Iranian intelligence services, whose representatives claimed that the assassins were acting without orders. The campaign against the reform-minded press hardened in February 1999 with the arrest of a moderate cleric, Mohsen Kadivar, whose writings conservatives saw as threatening.

Also in February, in elections for roughly 200,000 seats on village, town, and city councils, reformers once again won overwhelmingly, electing many women to office in rural areas. Vigorously debated was the antidemocratic nature of the office of the *rahbar*—the ranking cleric whose duties and authority are those usually equated with a head of state—and calls for its removal from the constitution now began to appear in the press.

In July students protested the closing of the *Salam* newspaper and opposed further restrictions on the press; and police, backed by a vigilante group known as Ansar-e Hezbollah, attacked a dormitory at Tehran University. Four students were reported killed, and hundreds more were injured or detained. On the day after the attack, 25,000 students staged a sit-in at the university and demanded the resignation of Tehran's police chief, whom they held responsible for the raid. Within 48 hours demonstrations had erupted in at least 18 major cities, including Gilan, Mashhad, and Tabriz in the north and Yazd, Esfahan, and Shiraz in the south. The demonstrators demanded that the murderers of the Farouhars and other intellectuals be brought to swift justice. They also called for freedom of the press, an increase in personal liberty, an end to the vigilante attacks on universities, and the release of 13 Iranian Jews who had been arrested by the government on allegations that they were spying for Israel. This was the first major student demonstration since the 1979 revolution, and it lasted for five days.

By mid-July, however, the government had quelled the protests, and hundreds more were arrested. In a temporizing settlement, Khatami criticized the students for rioting, but the security services were equally blamed for their ineptness and for having resorted to armed attacks on student lodgings. In the wake of the events in July, the chief of the Tehran police was dismissed from office, and there were calls for the resignation of the head of the national police force.

On February 18, 2000, more than 80 percent of the Iranian electorate voted in the first round of the election for members of the national legislature. In principle—with 75 percent of the elected deputies claiming adherence to the reformist group—Iranians had voted for more dynamic economic change and faster political liberalization. The only clear-cut outcome, however, was that the reformists, as a whole, won a majority of seats in the Majles. They remained divided among some 18 factions, however, and therefore represented a far-from-united front against the conservative establishment.

Even after a second round of elections, on May 5, when 66 seats were filled, there remained unsettled questions, particularly regarding 30 seats in Tehran. The Council of Guardians, which supervises Iran's elections, refused to validate those seats, so when the Majles convened on May 27, 41 seats were not yet allocated. Former President Rafsanjani finished last in the elections for Tehran, resigned from the legislature, and thereby abandoned his bid to become Speaker of the new Majles. The post of Speaker was taken instead by Mehdi Karrubi, a member of the Association of Combatant Clergy party and a junior member of the clergy who, though somewhat liberal, had close ties to the conservative establishment.

President Khatami ultimately obtained a liberal legislature but one that was not unified. Conservatives were content with having a sympathetic Speaker, a first deputy Speaker from their own ranks, and what was perhaps the most cohesive bloc within the Majles. (Moreover, the judiciary remained firmly in the hands of religious and political conservatives.) Consequently, the reformists faced an uphill struggle to advance their legislative program.

Political violence persisted. In the weeks leading to the 2000 elections, the presidential palace and other targets were hit by mortar fire. In the wake of the legislative elections, there was an assassination attempt made on Saeed Hajjarian, an important supporter of Khatami. Just as disruptive and threatening was a simultaneous burgeoning of attacks by extremists on newspapers and journals published by reformists. In mid-December liberal Culture Minister Ayatollah Mohajerani resigned, an event that was viewed as a severe blow to reform. Despite changes in the judiciary, the intimidation of the freethinking press by conservative groups and factions within the security services diminished only slightly during the year.

Activity in foreign relations was vigorous but not highly rewarding. Links with the United States improved with a loosening of U.S. economic sanctions in March 2000 and a visit to New York City by Khatami in early September, but no major breakthrough toward a final lifting of U.S. sanctions was apparent.

On January 13, 2001, a revolutionary court gave prolonged jail terms or heavy fines to 10 Iranian reformists who had participated in a proscribed conference in Berlin. The aggressive crackdown on reform-oriented Islamic factions and student groups culminated in March and April in the arrest of more than 60 eminent political figures associated with the banned Iran Freedom Movement (IFM). In addition, more reformist journals were closed down, and courts controlled by conservatives silenced more journalists. During the year, 60 reformers in the 290-member Majles were called before the courts on a variety of charges. In December a proreform member of parliament was sentenced to 13 months in jail for insulting the courts.

The hard-line offensive against the press and the reformists was part of a sustained campaign to frustrate Khatami and his cabinet, but it was also a tactic used to weaken the pro-Khatami wing of the government in advance of the June 8 presidential election. The election, however, proved a major success for Khatami. The president was reelected with an overwhelming 77 percent of the vote—an outcome that rebutted the conservative contention that Khatami and his followers had lost the support of the populace. Khatami's political platform was extremely modest, however, promising only to continue working within a formula of extreme moderation to pursue reform and move Iran toward democracy.

The new presidential term was expected to bring about significant strengthening of the reformist component within the Majles. Khatami declined as a matter of policy to confront the conservatives, and his postelection cabinet changed little from his original group of ministers. Indeed, the entire tone of policy in the wake of the June 2001 election was one of continued deference to conservative clerics, even on issues such as their introduction of regulations in midyear for the public flogging of persons found guilty of various social and religious offenses.

Opposition to and alienation from the conservative Islamic establishment was apparent during the presidential election when almost a third of the electorate opted not to vote. Active dissent was manifest in sporadic urban unrest. Officially reported cases included demonstrations in north Tehran against press controls, student protests in Tehran against the conservatives in January, and a major confrontation against the use of foreign labor at the 'Asaluyeh oil refinery in September.

In April there was an intensive Iranian missile attack on camps of an outlawed political party, the Mojahedin-e Khalq

Organization (Holy Warriors for the People, MKO) in Iraq, which indicated a continuing apprehension of MKO influence by the Iranian authorities.

Iran struggled to make headway in its key foreign policy aims, impeded by the domestic stalemate between the president and the conservatives. The United States renewed its Iran-Libya Sanctions Act in mid-2001 for five years. In June allegations were made in Washington that Iran had been involved in the 1996 bombing of the al-Khobar Towers in Saudi Arabia, which claimed the lives of 19 U.S. military personnel.

Although the Iranian leadership, notably Khatami, was quick to condemn the September 11 terrorist attacks in the United States, hopes that the campaign against terrorism would offer some degree of rapprochement with the United States were dimmed in late September when the Iranian leader (*rahbar*), Ali Khamenei, made an ardently anti-American speech. In the speech Khamenei explicitly rejected, except under a UN banner, Iranian participation in any actions against the Taliban government in Afghanistan, who were then sheltering al-Qaeda, the group behind the September 11 attacks, or in a global antiterrorist movement.

Iran was deeply affected by the State of the Union address by U.S. President George W. Bush on January 29, 2002, in which he denounced Iran's leading role in an "axis of evil." Senior officials in the Bush administration alleged that the Iranian government was sympathetic to the Taliban regime in Afghanistan and supportive of the al-Qaeda movement. For the rest of 2002, Bush and other key U.S. leaders continued to list Iran as a "rogue state" that supported terrorism, persisted in developing weapons of mass destruction, and deliberately impeded the Middle East peace process.

By early 2003, U.S. military forces occupied Iran's eastern and western neighbors. Under the specter of an attack by the United States once its Afghan and Iraqi campaigns had been completed, the Iranian regime was forced into a change in foreign policy. The established pattern of anti-American propaganda came to a temporary halt, and efforts were made to appease the United States. For example, the government shut the offices in Tehran of the virulently anti-American Hezb-e Eslami, an Afghan insurgent group led by Gulbuddin Hekmatyar. In response to international alarm that Iran was developing weapons of mass destruction, it was announced that an Iranian program to develop intermediate-range ballistic missiles would be curtailed, though other missile developments continued. Iran also rounded up al-Qaeda suspects, some of whom were handed over to Turkish authorities. Iranian support for terrorist groups, as defined by the United States, caused more difficulty in Tehran, where open links with Hezbollah and Hamas continued on the grounds that Iran defined them as Islamic independence organizations. Nonetheless, Iran's Ministry of Foreign Affairs for the first time publicly asserted that Iran would support any plan that would bring justice and peace to the Middle East.

The impact of strong U.S. policies on terrorism brought about a polarization of opinion within the Islamic regime. Until that point, debate on how to come to terms with the United States had been taboo. Thereafter, all but the extreme conservative Islamists took the view that talks with the United States had to become a priority, and even former leaders of the conservative Islamic factions within the regime, such as Rafsanjani, took the view that Iran could no longer simply ignore the United States.

A softening in the stance against negotiations with the United States assisted reformists and liberals within the regime to publish their own support for détente with Washington. The extreme Islamists, rather than giving ground, became even more entrenched in their determination to exclude the United States and vigorously resisted the domestic political reform and economic modernization programs implicit in Iran's coming to terms with the Bush administration. The deadlock between the Khatami government and the extreme conservatives became more intractable in the second half of 2002, effectively paralyzing domestic and foreign policy.

The deep divisions among the array of factions within Iran, principally those with conservative and reformist tendencies, persisted in 2003, and the clerical opponents of modernization grew in strength. Khatami suffered reverses following the dissolution of the Tehran City Council on January 14 and a poor performance in local elections on February 28, when there was a low turnout at the polls (a mere 12 percent in Tehran and 25 percent elsewhere) that was humiliating for the reform groups.

In March the Expediency Council ratified, in defiance of the president, a sizable increase in the budget of the Council of Guardians to fund that group's operations vetting nominees for the 2004 elections, an event that ensured the Council of Guardians' control over the selection of candidates. Khatami appeared to give up his program of modernization; he offered to accept a call in June from reformists for his resignation.

There was little respite in the crackdown on freedom of speech. In January of 2003, two newspapers were suspended by the conservative courts, and legal proceedings were instituted against a group of pollsters when the results of one of their public opinion polls flew in the face of conservative policy. The sentence of Hashem Aghajari, a history professor sentenced to death for apostasy in 2002, was commuted to four years in jail in July, but that was offset by continuing arrests of lawyers and newsmen. Fifteen members of the FMI were sent to prison in May. Internet access to foreign news on thousands of Web sites also was cut off, and the systematic jamming of satellite television channels began. Zahra Kazemi, a Canadian-Iranian journalist who was arrested for taking photographs outside a prison, died of head injuries while in custody in July. Canada condemned her death, and several members of the Iranian security services arrested in connection with the death were later exonerated.

In October Shirin Ebadi, an outspoken Iranian lawyer and human rights activist, was awarded the 2003 Nobel Prize for Peace.

Iranian foreign policy in 2003 was dominated by relations with the United States and events surrounding the U.S.-led coalition's invasion of Iraq. Iran accepted the fall of Iraqi President Saddam Hussein, supported the liberation of the Shi'ite communities in Iraq, and welcomed the disarming of MKO forces by the United States, but was disturbed by the U.S. occupation itself.

The situation was made more difficult by increasing evidence that the Iranian nuclear-development program included the production of weapons-grade nuclear material. In March of 2003, Khatami announced that a uranium-enrichment plant would be constructed near Esfahan to process local raw materials. Visits by the International Atomic Energy Agency (IAEA) later in the year confirmed that highly enriched uranium was present at two other locations. The IAEA called on Iran to prove by October 31 that it had not diverted materials to weapons use or face referral to the UN Security Council. Conservative factions opposed foreign intervention on this issue, but Foreign Minister Kamal Kharrazi offered in September to sign the additional safeguards to the Nuclear Nonproliferation Treaty, provided that the nuclear-enrichment program would be allowed to proceed. Russia, which was attempting to expand commercial links with Iran, aided in the construction of an Iranian nuclear station at Bushehr but concurred with the United States in opposing the station's use for military ends. The Iran-Libya Sanctions Act remained in effect in view of U.S. concerns over Iranian involvement in the acquisition of weapons of mass destruction and over its continuing support for terrorism.

The U.S. accused Iran of harboring al-Qaeda members suspected of involvement in the May attack on U.S. interests in Riyadh, Saudi Arabia. Iran acknowledged the activities of al-Qaeda personnel in the country but denied their connection with the terrorist incident in Riyadh. The European Union (EU) also fostered trade and investment in Iran. There were diplomatic skirmishes, however, on human rights that were not resolved, and the growing tensions over Iran's nuclear program caused further constraints on relations with the EU.

The Revolutionary Guards

Prior to the Islamic revolution of 1978–1979 in Iran, SAVAK (Organization of National Security and Information), the Iranian secret police and intelligence service, protected the regime of the shah by arresting, torturing, and executing many dissidents. After the shah's government fell, SAVAK and other intelligence services were eliminated and new services were created, though many low- and midlevel intelligence personnel were retained or rehired by the new services. The most important of the post-revolutionary intelligence services is the Ministry of Intelligence and Security (MOIS), which is responsible for both intelligence and counterintelligence. It also has conducted covert actions outside Iran in support of Islamic regimes elsewhere; for example, it was said to have provided military support to Muslim fighters in Kosovo and Bosnia and Herzegovina in the 1990s.

Shortly after the Islamic revolution, the new regime formed an impromptu militia known as the Revolutionary Guards (Pasdaran-e Enqelab), or simply as the Pasdaran, to forestall any foreign-backed coup—such as the one the CIA had undertaken to topple the nationalist Prime Minister Mohammad Mosaddeq in 1953—and to act as a foil to the powerful Iranian military. The Pasdaran also aided the country's new rulers in running the country and enforcing the government's Islamic code of morality. Only after Iraq invaded Iran in 1980 was the organization pressed into a broader role as a conventional military force; at the same time, the Pasdaran—which answered to its own independent ministry—sought to broaden its scope by developing departments for intelligence gathering (both at home and abroad) and clandestine activities. The names and functions of these departments are not well known. One such group, however, is known as the Qods (Jerusalem) Force. Like MOIS, it is responsible for conducting clandestine operations and for training and organizing foreign paramilitary groups in other parts of the Islamic world, including, purportedly, the Lebanese Shi'ite group Hezbollah. In the late 1990s agents of an organization associated with the Pasdaran were arrested and convicted of the murder of Iranian dissidents in Western Europe.

Reza Shah Pahlavi

Reza Shah Pahlavi.

Reza Khan (1878–1944), as he was originally known, was an Iranian military officer who rose through army ranks to become shah of Iran (1925–1941) and who began the modernization of his country.

Early Career

Reza was of a family of chiefs of a clan named Pahlevan. After the death of his father, Colonel Abbas Ali Khan, Reza's mother took him to Tehran, where he eventually enlisted as a private in an Iranian military unit under Russian instructors. Tall and powerfully built, the young soldier, from the beginning, showed an uncommonly strong will, remarkable intelligence, and a capacity for leadership. He was highly regarded by his seniors.

Coup of 1921

After centuries of misrule by its former rulers and the ravages of the war waged by foreign belligerents on its soil from 1914 to 1919, Iran in 1921 was prostrate, ruined, and on the verge of disintegration. The last of the shahs of the Qajar dynasty, Ahmad Shah, was young and incompetent, and the cabinet was weak and corrupt. Patriotic and nationalist elements had long been outraged at the domination of Iran by foreign powers, especially Britain and Russia, both of which had strong commercial and strategic interests in the country. This situation led Reza Khan to decide on an attempt at putting an end to the chaos by taking over power and forming a strong government, bolstered by an effective and disciplined military force. He contacted some young, progressive elements and on February 21, 1921, occupied Tehran at the head of 1,200 men. A young journalist, Sayyid Zia al-Din Tabataba'i, became prime minister, while Reza Khan took command of all the military forces and was appointed minister of war a few weeks after.

Reza Khan cherished the idea of modernizing and rebuilding Iran and leading it on the path of progress. Many had imagined that Reza Khan, whom they took to be an unsophisticated regimental officer, would be content with a high-sounding title and a sword of honor given by the shah. But Reza Khan was not about to step aside to allow a mixed group of inexperienced though sincere idealists and foreign-influenced opportunists to rule the country. His progress toward supreme power was extraordinarily rapid. Of a forbidding appearance, he talked very little and never revealed his intentions. Displaying great political talent against his opponents, he divided and weakened them. He also understood that to reach his ultimate objective he had to have complete control over a military force, and that required money. Able to levy some taxes, he built up the army with the proceeds and then used the army to collect more taxes, until finally he was able to gain control over the entire country. As war minister, he was the real power behind several prime ministers in succession until 1923, when he became prime minister himself.

The sovereign, Ahmad Shah, was ill and undergoing a lengthy treatment in Europe. In spite of the entreaties of Reza Khan and the Speaker of the Majles (parliament), the shah refused to return to Iran. Reza Khan then considered proclaiming a republic but was dissuaded by the strong opposition to the idea by the majority of the people. In 1925 the Majles deposed the absentee monarch, and a constituent assembly elected Reza Khan as shah, vesting sovereignty in the new Pahlavi dynasty.

Policies as Shah

After his coronation in April 1926, Reza Khan, now Reza Shah, continued the radical reforms he had embarked on while prime minister. He broke the power of Iran's tribes, which had been a turbulent element in the country, disarming them and settling some of the nomadic groups. In 1928 he put an end to the one-sided agreements and treaties that previous monarchs had signed with foreign powers, abolishing all special privileges. He built the Trans-Iranian Railway and started branch lines toward the principal cities (1927–1938). He emancipated women and required them to discard their veils (1935). He took control of the country's finances and communications, which up to then had been virtually in foreign hands. He built roads, schools, and hospitals and opened the first university (1934). His measures were directed at the same time toward the democratization of the country and its liberation from foreign interference.

His foreign policy, which had consisted essentially of playing the Soviet Union against Britain, failed when those two powers joined in 1941 to fight the Germans. To supply the

Soviet forces with war materials through Iran—the so-called Persian Corridor—the two allies jointly occupied the country in August 1941.

Reza Shah then decided to abdicate, to allow his son and heir, Mohammad Reza Pahlavi, to adopt a policy appropriate to the new situation, and to preserve his dynasty. He wanted to go to Canada, but the British government sent him first to Mauritius and then to Johannesburg, South Africa, where he died in July 1944.

Schools

Education in Iran is compulsory between the ages of 6 and 11. Roughly four-fifths of men and two-thirds of women are literate. Primary education is followed by a three-year guidance cycle, which assesses students' aptitudes and determines whether they will enter an academic, scientific, or vocational program during high school. Policy changes initiated since the revolution eliminated coeducational schools and required all schools and universities to promote Islamic values. The latter is a reaction to the strong current of Western secularism that permeated higher education under the monarchy. Adherence to the prevalent political dogma has long been an important factor for students and faculty who wish to succeed in Iranian universities. In fact, acceptance to universities in Iran is largely based on a candidate's personal piety, either real or perceived.

The University of Tehran was founded in 1934, and several more universities, teachers' colleges, and technical schools have been established since then. Iran's institutes of higher learning suffered after the revolution, however, when tens of thousands of professors and instructors either fled the country or were dismissed because of their secularism or association with the monarchy. Iran's universities have remained understaffed, and thus student enrollment has dropped in a country that greatly esteems higher education. The shortage of skilled teachers has led the government to encourage students to study abroad, in an effort to improve the quality and quantity of advanced degree holders and faculty. While overall enrollment numbers have fallen, the rate of women's admission at the university level has climbed dramatically, and by 2000 more than half of incoming students were women.

The public school system is controlled by the Ministry of Education and Training. Universities are under the supervision of the Ministry of Higher Education and Culture, and medical schools are under the Ministry of Health, Treatment, and Medical Education.

Shah 'Abbas I

Born into the Safavid dynasty, 'Abbas I—who was also known as 'Abbas the Great—succeeded his father, Muhammad, as shah (king) of Persia in 1587 and ruled until 1629. Under 'Abbas, the Safavid state reached its zenith. Tribal levies from Turkic tribes known as Kizilbash ("Red Heads," so named for their distinctive red, 12-sided headgear that announced their devotion to the 12 imams of Ithna 'Ashari Shi'ism) had been the military mainstay of the Safavids since they came to power. 'Abbas, however, saw their inherent fractious nature and formed the state's first standing army, which was modeled along European lines and consisted of troops (largely military slaves known as *ghulams*) who were loyal personally to the monarch. With this force, 'Abbas launched a series of campaigns in which he drove Ottoman and Uzbek troops from Iranian soil and shored up the country's borders.

He also promoted a more scholastic interpretation of Shi'ite doctrine, sidelining the more zealous and chiliastic manifestations of Shi'ite faith that had dominated under his predecessors, and opened many mosques and *madrasahs* (religious colleges). During his reign, religious divines gained influence at court and throughout society, a phenomenon that was to have powerful implications in later centuries. Moreover, under 'Abbas, the conversion of the population of Iran—once a bastion of Sunnism—to Shi'ism continued apace, and in many areas Shi'ism, the official doctrine under the Safavids, become predominant.

'Abbas made Esfahan Persia's capital, and under him it became one of the world's most beautiful cities. (The Maydan-e Emam [formerly the Maydan-e Shah, "King's Square"] is now a

UNESCO World Heritage site.) Persian artistic achievement reached a high point during his reign; illuminated manuscripts, ceramics, and painting all flourished, and the Portuguese, Dutch, and English competed for trade relations with Persia. Tolerant in public life (he granted privileges to Christian groups) and generally concerned for the people's welfare, 'Abbas could be cruel and mercurial with members of his own family and with those in his court.

Shah Isma'il

Isma'il was the religious and political leader who founded the Safavid dynasty and was shah (king) of Iran from 1501 to 1524. He made Shi'ism the official creed of Iran, which led to the eventual adoption of Shi'ism by the majority of Iranians. Isma'il's father, leader of a Shi'ite group known as the Kizilbash ("Red Heads," for their distinctive red, 12-sided hats that showed their adherence to the 12 imams of Ithna 'Ashari Shi'ism), died in battle against the Sunnis when Isma'il was only a year old. Isma'il was sent into hiding and emerged at the age of 14 to take his father's position as head of the Kizilbash. He quickly established a power base in northwestern Iran, and in 1501 he took the city of Tabriz and proclaimed himself shah of Iran. In a succession of swift conquests, he brought all of modern Iran and portions of present-day Iraq under his rule. In 1510, Isma'il defeated the Sunni Uzbek tribes and killed their leader, Muhammad Shaybani.

Isma'il declared Shi'ism the state creed, and the fact that his followers considered him a Muslim saint as well as monarch facilitated the process of conversion. Isma'il's action provoked the Ottoman Empire. Religious friction grew after the Ottoman sultan, Selim I, executed large numbers of his Shi'ite subjects as heretics and potential spies. In 1514 the Ottomans invaded northwest Iran and defeated Isma'il's army at the Battle of Chaldiran. Isma'il was wounded and nearly captured as he tried to rally troops. The warfare continued as a long series of border skirmishes, but Isma'il remained strong enough to prevent further inroads by the Ottomans. In 1517 he moved northwest, subduing the Sunni tribes in what is now Georgia. The basic conflict between the Shi'ite empire Isma'il had founded and the Sunni Ottomans in the west and the Sunni Uzbek tribes in the east continued for more than a century. Isma'il died at the age of 36, but the Safavid dynasty ruled Iran for two more centuries, until 1722.

Shari'ah

Because total and unqualified submission to the will of God is the fundamental tenet of Islam, Shari'ah (Islamic law) is the expression of God's command for Muslim society. It constitutes a system of duties that are incumbent upon a Muslim by virtue of his or her religious belief. In this light, canon law constitutes a divinely ordained path of conduct that guides Muslims toward a practical expression of their religious convictions in this world and the goal of divine favor in the world to come.

Under the 1979 Iranian constitution, all judges in Iran must base their decisions on the Shari'ah. In 1982 the Supreme Court struck down any portion of the law of the deposed monarchy that did not conform with the Shari'ah. In 1983 the Majles revised the penal code and instituted a system that embraced the form and content of Islamic law. This code implemented a series of traditional punishments, including retributions (Arabic *qisas*) for murder and other violent crimes—wherein the nearest relative of a murdered party may, if the court approves, take the life of the killer. Violent corporal punishments, including execution, are now the required form of chastisement for a wide range of crimes, ranging from adultery to alcohol consumption.

Muslim jurisprudence, the science of ascertaining the precise terms of the Shari'ah, is known as *fiqh* (literally "understanding"). It is generally accepted that the historical process of consolidating divine law within the Sunni community was completed by the end of the ninth century when the law had achieved a definitive formulation in a number of legal manuals written by different jurists. Throughout the medieval period this basic doctrine was elaborated and systematized in a large number of commentaries, and the voluminous literature thus produced constitutes the traditional textual authority of Shari'ah law. Generally speaking, the character of Shi'ite law does not differ greatly from that of the Sunni—the norms of behavior of the two communities differ only marginally. This was especially true in their early days, when the historic development of the sources of law was still incipient. Only later did Shi'ite legal theory begin to develop its own temper.

In classical form the Shari'ah differs from Western systems of law in two principal respects. First, the scope of the Shari'ah is much wider, since it regulates man's relationship not only with his neighbors and with the state, which is the limit of most other legal systems, but also with his God and his own conscience. Ritual practices, such as the daily prayers, almsgiving, fasting, and pilgrimage, are an integral part of Shari'ah law and usually occupy the first chapters in the legal manuals. The Shari'ah is also concerned as much with ethical standards as with legal rules, indicating not only what man is entitled or bound to do in law, but also what he ought, in conscience, to do or refrain from doing. Accordingly, certain acts are classified as praiseworthy (*mandub*), which means that their performance brings divine favor and their omission divine disfavor, and others as blameworthy (*makruh*), which means that omission brings divine favor and commission divine disfavor; but in neither case is there any legal sanction of punishment or reward, nullity or validity. The Shari'ah is not merely a system of law but also a comprehensive code of behavior that embraces both private and public activities.

The second major distinction between the Shari'ah and Western legal systems is the result of the Islamic concept of law as the expression of the divine will. When the Prophet Muhammad died in 632, Muslims felt that their communication with the divine will had also ceased so that the terms of the divine revelation were henceforth fixed and immutable. When, therefore, the process of interpretation and expansion of this source material was held to be complete with the crystallization of the doctrine in the medieval legal manuals, Shari'ah law became rigid and static. Unlike secular legal systems that grow out of society and change with the changing circumstances of society, Shari'ah law was imposed upon society from above. In Islamic jurisprudence it is not society that molds and fashions the law but the law that precedes and controls society.

Such a philosophy of law clearly poses fundamental problems for social advancement in contemporary Islam. How can the traditional Shari'ah law be adapted to meet the changing circumstances of modern Muslim society? This is the central issue in Islamic law in the modern world.

For the first Muslim community established under the leadership of the Prophet at Medina in 622, the Qur'anic revelations laid down basic standards of conduct. But the Qur'an is in no sense a comprehensive legal code. No more than 80 verses (of many hundreds in the Qur'an) deal with strictly legal matters; while these verses cover a wide variety of topics and introduce many novel rules, their general effect is simply to modify the existing Arabian customary law in certain important particulars.

During his lifetime Muhammad, as the supreme judge of the community, resolved legal problems as they arose by interpreting and expanding the general provisions of the Qur'an, and the same ad hoc activity was carried on after his death by the caliphs (temporal and spiritual rulers) of Medina. But the foundation of the Umayyad dynasty in 661, governing from its center in Damascus a vast military empire, sparked a greater development in the law. With the appointment of judges, or *qadi*s, to the various provinces and districts, an organized judiciary came into being. The *qadi*s were responsible for giving effect to a growing corpus of Umayyad administrative and fiscal law; and since they regarded themselves essentially as the spokesmen of the local law, elements and institutions of Roman-Byzantine and Persian-Sasanian law were absorbed into Islamic legal practice in the conquered territories. Depending upon the discretion of the individual *qadi*, decisions would be based upon the rules of the Qur'an where these were relevant; but the sharp focus in which the Qur'anic laws were held in the Medinian period had become lost with the expanding horizons of activity.

A reaction to this situation arose in the early eighth century when pious scholars, grouped together in loose, studious fraternities, began to debate whether Umayyad legal practice was properly implementing the religious ethic of Islam. Actively sponsored by the 'Abbasid rulers who came to power in the mid-eighth century pledged to build a truly Islamic state and society, the activities of the jurists (*faqih*, plural *fuqaha'*) in these early schools of law marked the real beginning of Islamic jurisprudence (at a time when clear distinctions between Sunni and Shi'ite did not yet exist). Their aim was to Islamize the law by reviewing the contemporary legal practice in the light of the Qur'anic principles and then, on this basis, adopting, modifying, or rejecting the practice as part of their ideal scheme of law.

Of the many early Sunni schools of law, the two most important were those of the Malikis in Medina and the Hanafis in Al-Kufah, named after two outstanding scholars in the respective localities, Malik ibn Anas and Abu Hanifah. Inevitably the Maliki and Hanafi doctrines, as they were then being recorded in the first compendiums of law, differed considerably from each other, not only because free juristic speculation was bound to produce varying results but also because the thought of the scholars was conditioned by their different social environments. A deep conflict of juristic principle emerged within the schools between those who maintained that outside the terms established in the Qur'an scholars were free to use their reason (*ra'y*) to ascertain the law and those who insisted that the only valid source of law outside the Qur'an lay in the precedents set by the Prophet himself.

The jurist al-Shafi'i (died 820) aimed to eliminate these schisms and produce greater uniformity in the law by expounding a firm theory of the sources from which the law must be derived. Al-Shafi'i's fundamental teaching was that knowledge of the Shari'ah could be attained only through divine revelation found either in the Qur'an or in the divinely inspired traditions (*sunnah*; from which stems the name Sunni derives) of the Prophet as ascertained through authentic reports (Hadith). Human reason in law should be strictly confined to the process of analogical deduction, or *qiyas*, problems not specifically answered by the divine revelation were to be solved by applying the principles upon which closely parallel cases had been regulated by the Qur'an or *sunnah*.

Al-Shafi'i's insistence upon the importance of the *sunnah* as a source of law produced a great activity in the collection and classification of Hadith, particularly among his own supporters, who formed what came to be known as the Shafi'i school, and the followers of Ahmad ibn Hanbal (died 855), who formed the Hanbali school. Sunni scholars maintained that six classical compilations of Hadith—especially those of Bukhari (died 870) and Muslim (died 875)—constituted an authentic record of the Prophet's precedents. Shi'ite scholars developed their own body of canonical Hadith literature, one that developed at a slower pace and consolidated at a later date than did the Sunni canon. These Hadith differ largely in their selection of sources, which are invariably associated, among the Ithna 'Ashari, with the Shi'ite imams. The general view of Western Orientalists, however, is that a considerable part of the Hadith tradition, whether Sunni or Shi'ite, represents the views of later jurists fictitiously or incorrectly ascribed to the Prophet in order to bestow greater authority upon a given doctrine.

Shafi'i's thesis formed the basis of the classical theory of the roots of jurisprudence (*usul al-fiqh*), which crystallized in the early 10th century. Juristic "effort" to comprehend the terms of the Shari'ah is known as *ijtihad*, and legal theory first defines the course that *ijtihad* must follow. In seeking the answer to a legal problem the jurist must first consult the Qur'an and the *sunnah*. Failing any specific solution in this divine revelation he must employ analogy (*qiyas*) or certain subsidiary principles of reasoning—*istihsan* (equitable preference) and *istislah* (the public interest). The legal theory then evaluates the results of *ijtihad* on the basis of the criterion of *ijma'* (consensus). As an attempt to define divine law, the *ijtihad* of individual scholars could result only in a tentative conclusion termed *zann* (conjecture). But where a conclusion became the subject of unanimous agreement by the qualified scholars, it became a certain (*yaqin*) and infallible expression of God's law.

Two major effects flowed from this classical doctrine of *ijma'*. It served first as a permissive principle to admit the validity of variant opinions as equally probable attempts to define the Shari'ah. Second, it operated as a restrictive principle to ratify the status quo; for once the *ijma'* had cast an umbrella authority not only over those points that were the subject of a consensus but also over existing variant opinions, to propound any further variant was to contradict the infallible *ijma'* and therefore was tantamount to heresy.

Ijma' set the final seal of rigidity upon the doctrine, and from the 10th century onward independent juristic speculation ceased. In the Arabic expression, "the door of *ijtihad* was closed." Henceforth jurists were *muqallid*s, or imitators, bound by the doctrine of *taqlid* (unquestioned acceptance) to follow the doctrine as it was recorded in the authoritative legal manuals.

Shari'ah law in its Sunni form is a candidly pluralistic system, the philosophy of the equal authority of the different schools being expressed in the purported dictum of the Prophet: "Difference of opinion among my community is a sign of the bounty of Allah." But outside the four schools of Sunni Islam stand the minority sects of the Shi'ah and the Ibadis (Kharijites), whose own versions of the Shari'ah differ considerably from those of the Sunnis. Shi'ite law in particular grew out of a fundamentally different politico-religious system in which the rulers, or imams, were held to be divinely inspired and therefore the spokesmen of the Lawgiver himself. The imamate ended in the late ninth century (when the last Imam, the "hidden Imam," purportedly went into occultation), and the interpretation of scriptures in Ithna 'Ashari Shi'ism (as practiced in Iran) fell to a body of Islamic scholars (*'ulama'*) who represented the hidden Imam. The absence of the hidden Imam led to a long discussion in the Shi'ite community—one that often turned vehement—in which the role of the *mujtahid*, in the form of the scholar of law, came to dominate. An entirely different standard of judicial discretion developed in the Shi'ite community. *Taqlid* continued to be the standard for the masses, but among the learned and erudite *'ulama'* in the community a system of scholarship developed in which the most learned earned the right of practicing *ijtihad*. The *mujtahid* became a source of great legal, religious, and (in some cases) political authority within Shi'ite communities.

Geographically, the divisions among the various schools and sects became fairly well defined as the *qadis*' courts in different areas became wedded to the doctrine of one particular school. Thus Hanafi law came to predominate in the Middle East and the Indian subcontinent; Maliki law in North, West, and Central Africa; Shafi'i law in East Africa, the southern parts of the Arabian Peninsula, Malaysia, and Indonesia; Hanbali law in Saudi Arabia, Shi'ite law in Iran and the Shi'ite communities of India and East Africa; and Ibadi law in Zanzibar, Oman, and parts of Algeria.

Although Shari'ah doctrine was all-embracing, Islamic legal practice has always recognized jurisdictions other than that of the *qadis*. Because the *qadis*' courts were hidebound by a cumbersome system of procedure and evidence, they did not prove a satisfactory organ for the administration of justice in all respects, particularly as regards criminal, land, and commercial law. Hence, under the broad head of the sovereign's administrative power (*siyasah*), competence in these spheres was granted to other courts, known collectively as *mazalim* courts, and the jurisdiction of the *qadis* was generally confined to private family and civil law. As the expression of a religious ideal, Shari'ah doctrine was always the focal point of legal activity, but it never formed a complete or exclusively authoritative expression of the laws that in practice governed the lives of Muslims.

Shari'ah duties are broadly divided into those that an individual owes to God (the ritual practices or *'ibadat*) and those that he owes to his fellow men (*mu'amalat*). It is the latter category of duties alone, constituting law in the Western sense, that is described here. These issues were defined at such an early date that there is little difference between Sunnis and Shi'ites in their application.

Offenses against the person, from homicide to assault, are punishable by retaliation (*qisas*), the offender being subject to precisely the same treatment as his victim. But this type of offense is regarded as a civil injury rather than a crime in the technical sense, since it is not the state but only the victim or his family who have the right to prosecute and to opt for compensation or blood money (*diyah*) in place of retaliation.

For six specific crimes the punishment is fixed (*hadd*): death for apostasy and for highway robbery; amputation of the hand for theft; death by stoning for extramarital sex relations (*zina*) where the offender is a married person and 100 lashes for unmarried offenders; 80 lashes for an unproved accusation of unchastity (*qadhf*) and for the drinking of any intoxicant.

Outside the *hadd* crimes, both the determination of offenses and the punishment therefore lie with the discretion of the executive or the courts.

The Islamic law of transactions as a whole is dominated by the doctrine of *riba*. Basically, this is the prohibition of usury, but the notion of *riba* was rigorously extended to cover, and therefore preclude, any form of interest on a capital loan or investment. And since this doctrine was coupled with the general prohibition on gambling transactions, Islamic law does not, in general, permit any kind of speculative transaction the results of which, in terms of the material benefits accruing to the parties, cannot be precisely forecast.

A patriarchal outlook is the basis of the traditional Islamic law of family relationships. Fathers have the right to contract their daughters, whether minor or adult, in compulsory marriage. Only when a woman has been married before is her consent to her marriage necessary; but even then the father, or other marriage guardian, must conclude the contract on her behalf. In Hanafi and Shi'ite law, however, only minor girls may be contracted in compulsory marriage, and adult women may conclude their own marriage contracts, except that the guardian may have the marriage annulled if his ward has married beneath her social status.

Husbands have the right of polygyny and may be validly married at the same time to a maximum of four wives. Upon marriage, a husband is obliged to pay to his wife her bride price (*mahr*), the amount of which may be fixed by agreement or by custom; and during the marriage he is bound to maintain and support her provided she is obedient to him, not only in domestic matters but also in her general social activities and conduct. A wife who rejects her husband's dominion by leaving the family home without just cause forfeits her right to maintenance.

But it is in the traditional law of divorce that the scales are most heavily weighted against the wife. A divorce may be effected simply by the mutual agreement of the spouses, which is known as *khul'* when the wife pays some financial consideration to the husband for her release; and according to all schools except the Hanafis a wife may obtain a judicial decree of divorce on the grounds of some matrimonial offense (e.g., cruelty, desertion, failure to maintain) committed by the husband. But the husband alone has the power unilaterally to terminate the marriage by repudiation (*talaq*) of his wife. *Talaq* is an extrajudicial process: a husband may repudiate his wife at will, and his motive in doing so is not subject to scrutiny by the court or any other official body. A repudiation repeated three times constitutes a final and irrevocable dissolution of the marriage, but a single pronouncement may be revoked at will by the husband during the period known as the wife's *'iddah*, which lasts for three months following the repudiation (or any other type of divorce) or, when the wife is pregnant, until the birth of the child. Shi'ites alone engage in the practice of *mut'ah* (literally, "pleasure"), or temporary marriage, an arrangement that has been the subject of derision by Sunnis (and even by some Shi'ites) as being little more than legalized prostitution. The practice simply involves a marriage, conducted under normal circumstances, for a contractually limited period of time—often for as little as a few days.

The legal position of children within the family group, as regards their guardianship, maintenance, and rights of succession, depends upon their legitimacy, and a child is legitimate only if he or she is conceived during the lawful wedlock of the parents. In Sunni law no legal relationship exists between a father and his illegitimate child, but there is a legal tie, for all purposes, between a mother and her illegitimate child. Guardianship of the person (e.g., control of education and marriage) and of the property of minor children belongs to the father or other close male, agnate relative, but the bare right of custody (*hadanah*) of young children whose parents are divorced or separated belongs to the mother or the female maternal relatives.

Traditionally, Shari'ah law was administered by the court of a single *qadi*, who was the judge of the facts as well as the law, although on difficult legal issues he might seek the advice of a professional jurist, or *mufti*. In fact, either party in a court dispute might visit a *mufti* and seek to obtain from him a *fatwa* (legal opinion). Neither the *qadi*, nor any other legal official, is bound by the *fatwa*. There was no hierarchy of courts and no organized system of appeals. Through his clerk (*katib*) the *qadi* controlled his court procedure, which was normally characterized by a lack of ceremony or sophistication. Legal representation was not unknown, but the parties would usually appear in person and address their pleas orally to the *qadi* while presenting, when admissible, any evidence or *fatwa*s they may have obtained.

The first task of the *qadi* was to decide which party bore the burden of proof. This was not necessarily the party who brought the suit, but was the party whose contention was contrary to the initial legal presumption attaching to the case. In the case of an alleged criminal offense, for example, the presumption is the innocence of the accused, and in a suit for debt the presumption is that the alleged debtor is free from debt. Hence the burden of proof would rest upon the prosecution in the first case and upon the claiming creditor in the second. This burden of proof might, of course, shift between the parties several times in the course of the same suit, as, for example, where an alleged debtor pleads a counterclaim against the creditor.

The standard of proof required, whether on an initial, intermediate, or final issue, was a rigid one and basically the same in both criminal and civil cases. Failing a confession or admission by the defendant, the plaintiff or prosecutor was required to produce two male witnesses to testify orally to their direct knowledge of the truth of his contention. Written evidence and circumstantial evidence, even of the most compelling kind, were normally inadmissible. Moreover, the oral testimony (*shahadah*) usually had to be given by two male, adult Muslims of established integrity or character. In certain cases, however, the testimony of women was acceptable (two women being required in place of one man), and in most claims of property the plaintiff could satisfy the burden of proof by one witness and his own solemn oath as to the truth of his claim.

If the plaintiff or prosecutor produced the required degree of proof, judgment would be given in his favor. If he failed to produce any substantial evidence at all, judgment would be given for the defendant. If he produced some evidence, but the evidence did not fulfill the strict requirements of *shahadah*, the defendant would be offered the oath of denial. Properly sworn, this oath would secure judgment in his favor; but if he refused it, judgment would be given for the plaintiff, provided, in some cases, that the latter himself would swear an oath.

In sum, the traditional system of procedure was largely self-operating. After his initial decision as to the incidence of the burden of proof, the *qadi* merely presided over the predetermined process of the law: witnesses were or were not produced, the oath was or was not administered and sworn, and the verdict followed automatically.

This system has continued, in one form or another, in various Islamic communities throughout the world. In countries such as Saudi Arabia, Shari'ah has continued as the rule of law since ancient times. Other countries, such as Egypt, have adopted Western-style law codes, only to later adapt various elements of Islamic law into their systems. Iran is the only modern Muslim country where the clergy have come to political power. Secular rules of law were largely abandoned after the Islamic revolution, and religious laws were reinstated. Moreover, continued refinement of legal-political thought through ongoing efforts of *ijtihad* culminated in the creation of a legal theory— pioneered by Ruhollah Khomeini—known as *velayat-e faqih* (governance by the religious jurist), which justifies the accrual of legal and political power into the hands of the clergy.

Shi'ites

Shi'ites are members of the smaller of the two major branches of Islam, distinguished from the majority Sunnis. In the 20th century the Sunnis constituted the majority of Muslims and formed majorities in most Muslim countries. Iran, however, is an overwhelmingly Shi'ite country (largest in terms of percentage of population and in overall numbers), with more than nine-tenths of Iranians being Shi'ites, mostly of the Ithna 'Ashari rite.

In early Islamic history the Shi'ites were a political faction (*shi'at 'ali*, "party of 'Ali") that supported the power of 'Ali, who was a cousin and son-in-law of Muhammad and was the fourth caliph (temporal and spiritual ruler) of the Muslim community. 'Ali was killed while trying to maintain his authority as caliph, and the Shi'ites gradually developed a religious movement that asserted the legitimate authority of 'Ali's lineal descendants, the 'Alids. This stand contrasted with that of the more pragmatic Sunni majority of Muslims, who were generally willing to accept the leadership of any caliph or caliphal dynasty whose rule afforded the proper exercise of religion and the maintenance of order in the Muslim world, particularly if that dynasty could trace its ancestry to Muhammad's tribe, the Quraysh.

Over the centuries the Shi'ite movement has deeply influenced all Sunni Islam, and its adherents numbered about 150 million in the early 21st century, or more than one-tenth of all Muslims.

In 656 'Ali had been raised to the caliphate with the support, among many others, of the murderers of the third caliph, 'Uthman. 'Ali never quite received the allegiance of all the Muslims, however, and thus had to wage increasingly unsuccessful wars to maintain himself in power. 'Ali was murdered in 661, and Mu'awiyah, his chief opponent and first of the Umayyad dynasty, became caliph. 'Ali's son al-Husayn later refused to recognize the legitimacy of Mu'awiyah's son and successor Yazid I as caliph. The Muslims of the Shi'ite-dominated town of Al-Kufah in Iraq, 'Ali's former capital, invited al-Husayn to become caliph. The Muslims in Iraq generally failed to support al-Husayn, despite their promises to do so, and he and his small band of followers were cut down (680) by the governor of Iraq's troops near Al-Kufah at the Battle of Karbala'. The city of Karbala' is now a pilgrimage spot for Shi'ites.

Swearing vengeance against the triumphant Umayyad government, the Kufans soon gained support from other groups that opposed the status quo—from aristocratic Muslim families of Medina, from pious men protesting a too-worldly interpretation of Islam, and from non-Arab Muslims (*mawali*), especially in Iraq, who demanded an equality denied them by the ruling Arabs. Over time the Shi'ites became a distinct collection of sects who were alike in their recognition of 'Ali and his descendants as the legitimate leaders of the Muslim community. The Shi'ites' conviction that the 'Alids should be the leaders of the Islamic world was never fulfilled over the centuries. But though the 'Alids never won power, 'Ali himself was recognized as a major hero of Sunni Islam, and his descendants by Fatimah, Muhammad's daughter, received the courtesy titles of "sayyids" and "sharifs."

The largest Shi'ite subdivision is that of the Ithna 'Ashari, or Twelvers, who recognize the legitimacy of a succession of twelve 'Alid claimants (beginning with 'Ali himself) who are known as imams. Other, smaller Shi'ite sects include the Isma'ili and the Zaydi.

Despite occasional Shi'ite rulers, the Shi'ites remained almost everywhere an Islamic minority until the start of the 16th century, when the Iranian Safavid dynasty under Shah Isma'il made it the sole legal faith of their empire, which then embraced the Persians of Iran, the Turks of Azerbaijan, and many of the Arabs of Iraq proper. These peoples have since been overwhelmingly of the Ithna 'Ashari rite. In the late 20th century, Shi'ite religious leadership became a major political force in Iran, where they toppled a secularist Pahlavi dynasty (1978–1979); in Lebanon, where they led resistance to Israeli occupation in the south during the 1980s and '90s; and in Iraq, where they were at the forefront of resistance against the Ba'thist regime of Saddam Hussein.

Sunni

A Sunni is a member of one of the two major branches of Islam, the branch that consists of the majority of that religion's adherents. Sunni Muslims regard their sect as the mainstream and traditionalist branch of Islam, as distinguished from the minority sect, the Shi'ites, and from several smaller groups.

In the early 21st century the Sunnis constituted the majority of Muslims in most Islamic countries, the most noteworthy exceptions being Iran, the largest Shi'ite country, and Iraq. They numbered about 900 million in the late 20th century and constituted nine-tenths of all the adherents of Islam.

The Sunnis recognize the first four caliphs as Muhammad's rightful successors, whereas the Shi'ites believe that Muslim leadership belonged to Muhammad's cousin/son-in-law, 'Ali, and his descendants alone. In contrast to the Shi'ites, the Sunnis have long conceived of the theocratic state built by Muhammad as an earthly, temporal dominion and have thus regarded the leadership of Islam as being determined not by divine order or inspiration but, largely, by the prevailing political realities of the Muslim world. This led historically to Sunni acceptance of the leadership of the foremost families of Mecca and to the acceptance of unexceptional caliphs, and even rule by marginally Muslim foreign interlopers, so long as their rule afforded the proper exercise of religion and the maintenance of order. The Sunnis accordingly held that the caliph must be a member of Muhammad's tribe, the Quraysh, but devised a theory of succession that was flexible enough to permit that allegiance be given to the de facto caliph, whatever his origins. The distinctions between the Sunnis and Shi'ites regarding the holding of spiritual and political authority remained firm even after the end of the caliphate itself in the 13th century.

The Sunnis' orthodoxy is marked by an emphasis on the views and customs of the majority of the community, as distinguished from the views of peripheral groups. The institution of consensus evolved by Sunni jurists allowed them to incorporate various customs and usages that arose through ordinary historical development but that had little or no roots in the Qur'an.

The Sunnis recognize the six "authentic" books of the Hadith, which contain the spoken tradition attributed to Muhammad. The Sunnis also accept as orthodox any of the four schools of Muslim law, Maliki, Shafi'i, Hanafi, or Hanbali.

Tehran

The city of Tehran, also spelled Teheran, is the capital of Iran and of Tehran Province. It is situated in the north-central part of the country on the southern slopes of the Elburz Mountains—which separate it from the Caspian Sea about 60 miles to the north—at an elevation of about 3,800 feet above sea level and between the Jajrud and the Karaj rivers. The central plateau of Iran extends to the south. The name Tehran is derived from the Old Persian *teh* ("warm") and *ran* ("place"). About 44 miles to the northeast rises the snow-covered peak of Mount Damavend, which rises to more than 18,000 feet and figures prominently in Persian legend. Tehran's population (1996) is 6,758,845, making

An aerial view of Tehran, set against the backdrop of the Elburz Mountains to the north.

it the largest city in Iran and one of the most populous cities in the world.

History

Tehran is the successor to the ancient Iranian capital of Ray (Rages), which was destroyed by the Mongols in AD 1220; traces of Ray—where the conqueror Alexander the Great halted while pursuing Darius III, king of Persia, in 330 BC—are still to be found south of Tehran. The village of Tehran is believed to have been a suburb of Ray in the fourth century, and after the fall of Ray many of the inhabitants moved to Tehran. The first European to mention Tehran was Don Ruy González de Clavijo, ambassador of the king of Castile to the court of the Turkic conqueror Timur (Tamerlane), who visited the town in 1404. Tehran was the home of several rulers of Persia's Safavid dynasty (1502–1736).

Tehran became prominent after its capture in 1785 by Agha Mohammad Khan, the founder of the Qajar dynasty (1794–1925), who made the city his capital in 1788. Since that date Tehran has been the capital of Iran. After the deposition of the last of the Qajars in 1925, the city was greatly expanded under Reza Shah Pahlavi (reigned 1925–1941). In 1943 the World War II leaders of the Allied Powers, representing the United States, the United Kingdom, and the Soviet Union, met at the Tehran Conference, at which, among other decisions, they guaranteed the independence of Iran.

During the reign of Mohammad Reza Shah Pahlavi (reigned 1941–1979) the city was rapidly modernized, partly the result of a booming petroleum industry. Following the overthrow of the shah in 1979, the city's development was hampered by economic difficulties resulting from the Iran-Iraq War, under-investment, and factional strife. Growth and modernization accelerated from the mid-1990s, in large part because of economic liberalization under President Mohammad Khatami.

Contemporary City

Tehran experiences warm summers and relatively cool winters. High and low mean monthly temperatures are 84°F in July and 39°F in January, although there are fluctuations in temperature within the city, particularly between the arid south and the cooler northern neighborhoods, which rise into the foothills of the Elburz Mountains. The average annual precipitation is about 8 inches; rain usually falls from November to the end of May, and snow also occurs from December to the end of February. Air pollution has worsened as a result of the increase in motor traffic and the increased use of fuel oil by industry.

The ethnic composition of Tehran is similar to that of Iran in general. The overwhelming majority of the inhabitants are Muslim, mostly Shi'ites, but there are also small groups of Christians, Jews, and Zoroastrians. Persian is the language in general use, but approximately one-fourth of the population speaks Azerbaijani, a language closely related to Turkish.

Niavaran Palace, Tehran.

Instability in neighboring countries since the 1980s has contributed to an increase in the immigrant population of the city,
particularly in the number of refugees from Afghanistan.

Because it has grown rapidly since 1925, Tehran, of all Iranian cities, has the least Oriental aspect. Since the 1950s a number of medium- and high-rise buildings have been constructed.
The fashionable districts of the city are to the north, and the old
town and the bazaar are to the south. Important buildings
include the Motahari (formerly Sepahsalar) Mosque, the
Baharstan Palace (the seat of the Majles, or parliament), the
Shams al-Emareh, and the Niavaran Palace. The Golestan
Palace (containing the famous peacock throne and the jewel-
studded Naderi throne), the Sa'adabad Palace, and the Marmar
(Marble) Palace are now maintained as museums. There is also a
notable archaeological museum and an ethnographical museum.
Tehran is the seat of the University of Tehran (1934), the Iran
University of Science and Technology (1928), and several other
institutions of higher learning.

More than half of Iran's manufactured goods are produced
in Tehran. Industrial plants manufacture such items as textiles,
cement, sugar, chinaware and pottery, electrical equipment, and
pharmaceuticals. There is also a car-assembly industry, and an
oil refinery is in operation at Ray.

Three paved roads run northward, one to the west, two to
the south, and one to the east. The Iranian state railway has lines
running north, northwest, south, and east from Tehran; the city
is also linked to the trans-Europe railway system via Turkey. The
Tehran Metro—one of the few subway systems in the Middle
East—connects various parts of the city and connects Tehran to
adjacent suburbs.

Tehran is connected by air to major cities in Europe and
Asia and to states in the Persian Gulf. Domestic air services also
link the capital to major Iranian towns. There is an international
airport at Mehrabad, 6 miles west of central Tehran; two smaller
airports—at Qal'eh Morghi and Daushan-Tapeh—are used by
small aircraft.

The United Nations

The main function of the United Nations, established in 1945, is to preserve international peace and security. Chapter 6 of the UN Charter provides for the pacific settlement of disputes, through the intervention of the Security Council, by means such as negotiation, mediation, arbitration, and judicial decisions. The Security Council may investigate any dispute or situation to determine whether it is likely to endanger international peace and security. At any stage of the dispute, the council may recommend appropriate procedures or methods of adjustment, and if the parties fail to settle the dispute by peaceful means, the council may recommend terms of settlement.

The Security Council consists of five permanent members—the United States, China, France, the United Kingdom, and the Russian Federation—plus 10 nonpermanent members.

The nonpermanent members are chosen to achieve equitable regional representation, five members coming from Africa or Asia, one from Eastern Europe, two from Latin America, and two from Western Europe or other areas. Five of the 10 nonpermanent members are elected each year by the General Assembly for two-year terms, and five retire each year. The presidency is held by each member in rotation for one month.

Each Security Council member is entitled to one vote. On all "procedural" matters—the definition of which is sometimes in dispute—decisions by the council are made by an affirmative vote of any nine of its members. Substantive matters, such as the investigation of a dispute or the application of sanctions, also require nine affirmative votes, including those of the five permanent members holding veto power. In practice, however, a permanent member may abstain without impairing the validity of the decision. A vote on whether a matter is procedural or substantive is itself a substantive question. Because the Security Council is required to function continuously, each member is represented at all times at the UN's headquarters in New York City.

The goal of collective security, whereby aggression against one member is met with resistance by all, underlies Chapter 7 of the UN Charter, which grants the Security Council the power to order coercive measures—ranging from diplomatic, economic, and military sanctions to the use of armed force—in cases where attempts at a peaceful settlement have failed. Such measures were seldom applied during the Cold War, however, because tensions between the United States and the Soviet Union prevented the Security Council from agreeing on the instigators of aggression. Instead, actions to maintain peace and security often took the form of preventive diplomacy and peacekeeping. In the post–Cold War period, appeals to the UN for peacekeeping and related activities increased dramatically, and new threats to international peace and security were confronted, including AIDS and international terrorism.

International armed forces were first used in 1948 to observe cease-fires in Kashmir and Palestine. Although not specifically mentioned in the UN Charter, the use of such forces as a buffer between warring parties pending troop withdrawals and negotiations—a practice known as peacekeeping—was formalized in 1956 during the Suez Crisis involving Egypt, Israel, France, and the United Kingdom. Peacekeeping missions have taken many forms, though they have in common the fact that they are designed to be peaceful, that they involve military troops from several countries, and that the troops serve under the authority of the UN Security Council. In 1988 the UN Peacekeeping Forces were awarded the Nobel Prize for Peace.

During the Cold War, so-called first-generation, or "classic," peacekeeping was used in conflicts in the Middle East and Africa and in conflicts stemming from decolonization in Asia. Between 1948 and 1988 the UN undertook 13 peacekeeping missions involving generally lightly armed troops from neutral countries other than the permanent members of the Security Council—most often Canada, Sweden, Norway, Finland, India, Ireland, and Italy. Troops in these missions, the so-called Blue Helmets, were allowed to use force only in self-defense. The missions were given and enjoyed the consent of the parties to the conflict and the support of the Security Council and the troop-contributing countries.

With the end of the Cold War, the challenges of peacekeeping became more complex. In order to respond to situations in which internal order had broken down and the civilian population was suffering, "second-generation" peacekeeping was developed to achieve multiple political and social objectives. Unlike first-generation peacekeeping, second-generation peace-keeping often involves civilian experts and relief specialists as well as soldiers. Another difference between second-generation and first-generation peacekeeping is that soldiers in some second-generation missions are authorized to employ force for reasons other than self-defense. Because the goals of second-generation peacekeeping can be variable and difficult to define, however, much controversy has accompanied the use of troops in such missions.

In the 1990s, second-generation peacekeeping missions were undertaken in Cambodia (1991–1993), the former Yugoslavia (1992–1995), Somalia (1992–1995), and elsewhere and included troops from the permanent members of the Security Council as well as from the developed and developing world (e.g., Australia, Pakistan, Ghana, Nigeria, Fiji, and India).

In the former Yugoslav province of Bosnia and Herzegovina, the Security Council created "safe areas" to protect the predominantly Bosniac (Bosnian Muslim) population from Serbian attacks, and UN troops were authorized to defend the areas with force. In each of these cases, the UN reacted to threats to peace and security within states, sometimes taking sides in domestic disputes and thus jeopardizing its own neutrality.

Between 1988 and 2000 more than 30 peacekeeping efforts

were authorized, and at their peak in 1993 more than 80,000 peacekeeping troops representing 77 countries were deployed on missions throughout the world. In the first years of the 21st century, annual UN expenditures on peacekeeping operations exceeded $2 billion.

By subscribing to the UN Charter, all members undertake to place at the disposal of the Security Council armed forces and facilities for military sanctions against aggressors or disturbers of the peace. During the Cold War, however, no agreements to give this measure effect were concluded. Following the end of the Cold War, the possibility of creating permanent UN forces was revived.

During the Cold War the provisions of Chapter 7 of the UN Charter were invoked only twice with the support of all five permanent Security Council members—against Southern Rhodesia in 1966 and against South Africa in 1977. After fighting broke out between North and South Korea in June 1950, the United States obtained a Security Council resolution authorizing the use of force to support its ally South Korea and turn back North Korean forces. Because the Soviet Union was at the time boycotting the Security Council over its refusal to seat the People's Republic of China, there was no veto of the U.S. measure. As a result, a U.S.-led multinational force fought under the UN banner until a cease-fire was reached on July 27, 1953.

The Security Council again voted to use UN armed forces to repel an aggressor following the August 1990 invasion of Kuwait by Iraq. After condemning the aggression and imposing economic sanctions on Iraq, the council authorized member states to use "all necessary means" to restore "peace and security" to Kuwait. The resulting Persian Gulf War lasted six weeks, until Iraq agreed to comply with UN resolutions and withdraw from Kuwait. The UN continued to monitor Iraq's compliance with its resolutions, which included the demand that Iraq eliminate its weapons of mass destruction. In accordance with this resolution, the Security Council established a UN Special Mission (UNSCOM) to inspect and verify Iraq's implementation of the cease-fire terms. The United States, however, continued to bomb Iraqi weapons installations from time to time, citing Iraqi violations of "no-fly" zones in the northern and southern regions of the country, the targeting of U.S. military aircraft by Iraqi radar, and the obstruction of inspection efforts undertaken by UNSCOM.

The preponderant role of the United States in initiating and commanding UN actions in Korea in 1950 and the Persian Gulf in 1990–1991 prompted debate over whether the requirements and spirit of collective security could ever be achieved apart from the interests of the most powerful countries and without U.S. control. The continued U.S. bombing of Iraq subsequent to the Gulf War created further controversy about whether the raids were justified under previous UN Security Council resolutions and, more generally, about whether the United States was entitled to undertake military actions in the name of collective security without the explicit approval and cooperation of the UN. Meanwhile, some military personnel and members of the U.S. Congress opposed the practice of allowing U.S. troops to serve under UN command, arguing that it amounted to an infringement of national sovereignty. Still others in the United States and Western Europe urged a closer integration of United States and allied command structures in UN military operations.

In order to assess the UN's expanded role in ensuring international peace and security through dispute settlement, peacekeeping, peace-building, and enforcement action, a comprehensive review of UN Peace Operations was undertaken. The resulting Brahimi Report (formally the Report of the Panel on United Nations Peace Operations), issued in 2000, outlined the need for strengthening the UN's capacity to undertake a wide variety of missions. Among the many recommendations of the report was that the UN maintain brigade-size forces of 5,000 troops that would be ready to deploy in 30 to 90 days and that UN headquarters be staffed with trained military professionals able to use advanced information technologies and to plan operations with a UN team including political, development, and human rights experts.

The UN's founders hoped that the maintenance of international peace and security would lead to the control and eventual reduction of weapons. Therefore the UN Charter empowers the General Assembly to consider principles for arms control and disarmament and to make recommendations to member states and the Security Council. The UN Charter also gives the Security Council the responsibility to formulate plans for arms control and disarmament. Although the goals of arms control and disarmament have proved elusive, the UN has facilitated the negotiation of several multilateral arms control treaties.

Because of the enormous destructive power realized with the development and use of the atomic bomb during World War II, the General Assembly in 1946 created the Atomic Energy Commission to assist in the urgent consideration of the control of atomic energy and in the reduction of atomic weapons.

In 1947 the Security Council organized the Commission for Conventional Armaments to deal with armaments other than weapons of mass destruction, but progress on this issue also was blocked by disagreement between the Soviet Union and the Western powers. As a result, in 1952 the General Assembly voted to replace both of these commissions with a new Disarmament Commission. Consisting of the members of the Security Council and Canada, this commission was directed to prepare proposals that would regulate, limit, and balance reduction of all armed forces and armaments; eliminate all weapons of mass destruction; and ensure international control and use of atomic energy for peaceful purposes only. After five years of vigorous effort and little progress, in 1957 the International Atomic Energy Agency was established to promote the peaceful uses of atomic energy.

In 1961 the General Assembly adopted a resolution declaring the use of nuclear or thermonuclear weapons to be contrary to international law, to the UN Charter, and to the laws of humanity. Two years later, on August 5, 1963, the Nuclear Test-Ban Treaty was signed by the Soviet Union, the United Kingdom, and the United States. The treaty—to which more than 150 states later adhered—prohibited nuclear tests or explosions in the atmosphere, in outer space, and underwater. In 1966 the General Assembly unanimously approved a treaty prohibiting the placement of weapons of mass destruction in orbit, on the Moon, or on other celestial bodies and recognizing the use of outer space exclusively for peaceful purposes.

In June 1968 the General Assembly approved the Treaty on the Nonproliferation of Nuclear Weapons, which banned the spread of nuclear weapons from nuclear to nonnuclear powers; enjoined signatory nonnuclear powers, in exchange for technical assistance in developing nuclear power for "peaceful purposes," not to develop or deploy nuclear weapons; and committed the nuclear powers to engage in measures of disarmament.

The UN has been active in attempting to eliminate other weapons of mass destruction of a variety of types and in a variety of contexts.

In 1993 the Chemical Weapons Convention, which prohibited the development, production, stockpiling, and use of chemical weapons and called for the destruction of existing stockpiles within 10 years of the treaty entering into force (1997), was opened for signature.

In 1996 the Comprehensive Nuclear Test-Ban Treaty, which prohibited the testing of nuclear weapons, was signed—though it has not yet entered into force—and two years later a treaty banning the production and export of antipersonnel land mines (Convention on the Prohibition of the Use, Stockpiling, Production, and Transfer of Antipersonnel Mines and on Their Destruction) was concluded. Despite international pressure, the United States refused to sign both the test-ban and the land-mine agreements.

A CLOSER LOOK

The UN Security Council

by Edward C. Luck

The UN Security Council's irresolute wrangling in 2003 over whether to use force in Iraq spurred pointed questioning by many observers about its relevance and even its future. Continuing differences over the course of postwar reconstruction only added to the chorus of doubts. On one point the world body's most fervent admirers and detractors seemed to agree: the Security Council was in serious, perhaps critical, condition. "Events have shaken the international system," warned UN Secretary-General Kofi Annan. If the UN's principal organs—beginning with the Security Council—"are to regain their authority, they may need radical reform," he said.

Perhaps, as Annan warned, the world body is—once again—at a crossroads. Before sharpening their scalpels in preparation for radical reform, however, the member states should ask whether the diagnosis of the malady is, in fact, correct. A second opinion, or at least a quick historical review, would be in order before reserving the operating room.

The United Nations was established in 1945, largely on U.S. initiative, to maintain international peace and security. The key Security Council was granted unprecedented legal and enforcement powers under Chapter 7 of the UN Charter to ensure that its decisions would be respected and implemented by all member states. On the other hand, the charter granted the leaders of the victorious World War II coalition—the United States, the Soviet Union, the United Kingdom, China, and France—veto power over the Security Council's substantive decisions. This was seen as a way to both protect their individual interests and help perpetuate the wartime alliance, a key goal. These provisions were soon put to a severe test.

When the alliance gave way to the Cold War just a few years after the UN's founding conference in San Francisco, Moscow began to cast veto after veto, and the Security Council was paralyzed for much of the next four decades. Critics, particularly from the U.S. Congress, questioned the utility of a council that was so fundamentally divided. Many called for the elimination of the veto, but the founders had placed the bar for amending the charter—ratification by all five permanent members and two-thirds of the membership as a whole—very high so that their original architecture could withstand shifts in political fortunes. As large numbers of newly independent states from Africa and Asia joined the world body, it was the United States that came to rely on its right to block disagreeable council actions. Over the UN's first quarter century, the United States did not exercise a single veto, but after 1970 it exercised its veto power substantially more often than any of the other four permanent members.

Following the end of the Cold War, the Security Council rediscovered Chapter 7 and began to act more decisively to protect world security. During the 1990s it passed a record number of enforcement, peacekeeping, and nation-building measures. For example, it authorized a U.S.-led military coalition to expel Iraqi forces that had invaded Kuwait in 1991, imposed damaging economic sanctions on Baghdad, and mandated unusually intrusive inspections of Iraqi weapons development. For more than a decade, Iraqi President Saddam Hussein responded with islands of cooperation amid a sea of defiance, a policy that time and again left the Security Council members divided about how to proceed. It was thus hardly surprising that the council members were unable to endorse the use of force against Iraq in 2002–2003, despite President George W. Bush's repeated contention that the very credibility of the council was at stake. To the president's critics, the U.S.-U.K. decision to intervene militarily without the explicit authorization of the Security Council represented what Annan called "a fundamental challenge to the principles on which, however imperfectly, world peace and stability have rested for the last 58 years." Clearly the rift over the council's proper role in international security matters remained as wide as ever.

The United States had never accepted that it could use force only with the Security Council's approval. By their actions over the decades, other countries had made it clear that they, too, reserved this prerogative for themselves. Prior council approval of military action had rarely been sought and had infrequently been granted. Of the hundreds of uses of force by various member states since 1945, only a handful had been graced with council sanction. Even Annan had argued that when the council is deadlocked over the use of force to relieve a humanitarian calamity, as in the case of Kosovo in 1999, it may be morally, if not legally, justifiable to act outside the UN Charter.

The member states, it seemed, had some significant differences of perspective and values to sort out. But is the nature of the council's current malaise primarily institutional or political? Would the cure lie in reshaping the composition and rules of the council or in addressing the evident political differences among the member states? Should the locus of the surgery, in other words, be within the walls of the Security Council chamber or in national capitals? At this juncture, misdiagnosing what ails the council could well risk transforming the claim of its irrelevance into a self-fulfilling prophecy.

For a decade now the UN member states—now numbering 191—have been engaged in a vigorous and inconclusive debate about what a reformed Security Council should look like. It is widely accepted that the council should be enlarged from 15 to 20 to 25 members, in part to correct a perceived underrepresentation of less-developed countries. Perhaps five of these seats would go to new permanent members. Most observers call for greater transparency and accountability in the council's decision-making and either constraints on or the elimination of the veto. Yet these same voices insist that, in the name of equity, any new permanent members should have the same veto powers as the original five. Under this recipe for gridlock, any one of as many as 10 countries could block, or threaten to block, council action.

All of this is moot, of course, as long as the member states remain divided over which states should be named to the council. Indeed, the very factor that prompted Annan's plea for radical reform—the political crisis within the council—suggested that the prospects for reaching agreement were even worse today than they were in the mid-1990s, when the last reform push took place. Perversely, for this we should be thankful; the core problem is strategic, not institutional. It hinges on Security Council relations with the United States, not with the less-developed world. As the 2003 war in Iraq demonstrated, U.S. military capacities far surpass those of other council members, and the gap is widening. Since the terrorist attacks of September 11, 2001, Americans also feel far more vulnerable to terrorist attacks and, hence, less inclined to place their national defense in the hands of non-Americans. This combination foreshadows both future splits within the council and the likelihood that the United States would consider military options outside the framework of a deadlocked Security Council.

The good news is that a Security Council that could survive the ideological struggles of the Cold War is likely to find ways of adapting to these new political challenges. Even in the midst of the bitter debate over Iraq, the council members managed to find common ground on acute crises in other parts of the world. The bad news is that those who pressed for an enlargement of the council and limitations on the veto, in part to counterbalance American influence, were running the risk of creating an organ that was even less reflective of the balance of power outside the organization. This would likely encourage the very trends toward unilateralism in Washington that could eventually undermine the political and strategic foundation of the world body. Part of this foundation from the outset, it should be recalled, was the centrality of American power and vision for the global enterprise. Building a stronger bridge between Washington and Turtle Bay is where reform should begin.

Edward C. Luck is professor of practice in international and public affairs and director of the Center on International Organization at the School of International and Public Affairs at Columbia University, New York City. He is the author of Mixed Messages: American Politics and International Organization, 1919–1999 *(1999).*

Weapons of Mass Destruction (WMD)

Broadly speaking, a weapon of mass destruction (WMD) is any weapon with the capacity to inflict death and destruction on such a massive scale and so indiscriminately that its very presence in the hands of a hostile power can be considered a grievous threat. Modern weapons of mass destruction are either nuclear, biological, or chemical weapons—frequently referred to collectively as NBC weapons.

The continued search in 2003 for WMD in Iraq heightened international curiosity about them. The term "weapons of mass destruction" has been in use since at least 1937, when newspapers described German bomber aircraft as "weapons of mass destruction" because they were being used to raze Republican-held cities during the Spanish Civil War. During the Cold War, WMD was narrowly defined to include only nuclear weapons because their use threatened the entire planet. By the end of the 1990–1991 Persian Gulf War, WMD had been used in United Nations Security Council Resolution 687—which imposed on Iraq strict rules for disarmament—to describe nuclear, biological, and chemical weapons. Since that time others have tried to alter the definition to include any weapon that disperses radioactivity or causes mass panic.

Nuclear weapons are thus far the most devastating weapons of mass destruction. They inflict their damage by a combination of intense blast, heat, electromagnetic energy, and radioactivity. Within a few minutes the single rudimentary bomb dropped on Hiroshima in August 1945 killed tens of thousands of people and destroyed all the buildings inside a 1-mile radius of "ground zero" (i.e., the point of impact). Nuclear weapons get their explosive power from a sustained nuclear chain reaction involving fission (the splitting of atoms) or fusion (the combining of lighter atoms to form new, heavier ones). Creating such a chain reaction requires either highly enriched uranium (HEU) or plutonium. Plutonium occurs very rarely in nature and must be made inside a nuclear reactor. Uranium ore contains about 0.7 percent U-235 (the isotope needed to sustain an explosive chain reaction) and must be refined until the U-235 content is at least 90 percent.

About 110 pounds of highly enriched uranium or 22 pounds of plutonium are needed to build a crude nuclear bomb. To acquire even these small amounts, one requires a sophisticated enrichment plant or a nuclear reactor and reprocessing facility to extract plutonium; alternatively, one could acquire highly enriched uranium or plutonium from someone with such facilities.

The cornerstones of the effort to control the spread of nuclear weapons materials and technologies are the Treaty on the Nonproliferation of Nuclear Weapons (NPT), which has nearly 200 member states and came into force in 1970, and the Comprehensive Nuclear Test-Ban Treaty (CTBT), which still requires signature by India, Pakistan, and North Korea. Before it can come into force, nine other countries, including the United States, must ratify the CTBT. The International Atomic Energy Agency (IAEA), established under the auspices of the United Nations in 1957, helps ensure that states live up to their NPT obligations.

During World War I both the German and the Allied armies used chemical weapons (CW) as a means of breaking the deadlock of trench warfare. By war's end in 1918, approximately 1 million soldiers and civilians had been injured by this type of weapon, and nearly 100,000 had died. More recently, CW were used during the 1980–1990 war between Iran and Iraq, most often by the Iraqis, who were trying to overcome the numerical superiority of the Iranian army. CW are divided into four categories:

- Choking agents, such as chlorine and phosgene gas, are the oldest and the easiest to manufacture. These have a corrosive effect on the lining of the lungs, causing fluid buildup, but they can easily be defended against by wearing a gas mask.

- Blood agents, such as hydrogen cyanide and cyanogen chloride gas, work by preventing red blood cells from absorbing oxygen and transmitting it throughout the body.

- Blister agents attack any exposed area of the body, and to defend against them personnel must wear cumbersome protective clothing as well as a gas mask. Mustard gas (sulfur mustard) and lewisite are examples of blister agents.

- Nerve agents were developed in the 1930s to be more lethal and faster-acting than previous types of CW. They are absorbed through the skin or lungs and within seconds will disrupt the transmission of nerve signals to and from the brain. These agents include sarin, tabun, and VX.

Controlling the proliferation of CW is difficult because many of the chemicals involved in their production also have nonmilitary uses. For example, thiodiglycol is used to make mustard gas but is also an ingredient in ink for felt-tip pens.

The Chemical Weapons Convention is the first international treaty intended to eliminate an entire category of WMD. The treaty came into force in 1997, and member states have 10 years to eliminate their CW stockpiles and any related infrastructure. The treaty established the Organization for the Prohibition of Chemical Weapons to monitor and ensure its provisions. This is done through a series of rigorous scheduled and short-notice inspections of known or suspected CW facilities and through the investigation of incidents of alleged use.

Biological weapons (BW) encompass pathogens (bacteria,

viruses, and fungi) that cause diseases and toxins that are derived from organisms such as plants, snakes, and insects. Anthrax and smallpox are examples of pathogens. An example of a toxin is ricin, which is derived from the seed of the castor bean. Crude forms of biological warfare have been used since ancient times, when the decaying corpses of animals and humans were placed near enemy food and water supplies with the intention of spreading disease. In the 18th century the British distributed blankets contaminated with smallpox to decimate the Indian tribes with which they were warring. During World War II the Japanese used various BW agents against the Chinese. Britain, the Soviet Union, and the United States all had significant BW programs during the Cold War.

BW pose a special problem for arms controllers, because most of the equipment and materials used in their production also have peaceful commercial uses. There is very little observable difference between a BW factory and a medical research facility or pharmaceutical plant. The Biological and Toxin Weapons Convention bans all BW and their production facilities. It has over 140 member states and has been in force since 1975. Its members, however, have been unable to agree on how to verify the treaty. In 2001 the United States pulled out of talks to reach a verification protocol, in part over concerns that the proposed inspections would be so intrusive as to threaten the security of proprietary information owned by pharmaceutical companies.

The White Revolution (1963)

The period 1960–1963 marked a turning point in the development of the Iranian state. Industrial expansion was promoted by the Pahlavi regime, while political parties that resisted the shah's absolute consolidation of power were silenced and pushed to the margins. In 1961 the shah dissolved the 20th Majles and cleared the way for the land reform law of 1962. Under this program, the landed minority was forced to give up ownership of vast tracts of land for redistribution to small-scale cultivators. The former landlords were compensated for their loss in the form of shares of state-owned Iranian industries. Cultivators and workers were also given a share in industrial and agricultural profits, and cooperatives began to replace the large landowners in rural areas as sources of capital for irrigation, agrarian maintenance, and development.

The land reforms were mere preludes to the shah's "White Revolution," a far more ambitious program of social, political, and economic reform. Put to a plebiscite and ratified in 1963, these reforms eventually redistributed land to some 2.5 million families, established literacy and health corps to benefit Iran's rural areas, further reduced the autonomy of tribal groups, and advanced social and legal reforms that furthered the emancipation and enfranchisement of women. In subsequent decades, per capita income for Iranians skyrocketed, and oil revenue fueled an enormous increase in state funding for industrial development projects.

The new policies of the shah did not go unopposed, however; many Shi'ite leaders criticized the White Revolution, holding that liberalization laws concerning women were against Islamic values. More important, the shah's reforms chipped away at the traditional bases of clerical power. The development of secular courts had already reduced clerical power over law and jurisprudence, and the reforms' emphasis on secular education further eroded the former monopoly of the *'ulama'* in that field. (Paradoxically, the White Revolution's Literacy Corps was to be the only reform implemented by the shah to survive the Islamic revolution, because of its intense popularity.) Most pertinent to clerical independence, land reforms initiated the breakup of huge areas previously held under charitable trust (*vaqf*). These lands were administered by members of the *'ulama'* and formed a considerable portion of that class's revenue.

In 1963 a relatively obscure member of the *'ulama'* named Ruhollah Musawi Khomeini—a professor of philosophy at the Fayziyyeh Madrasah in Qom who was accorded the honorific ayatollah—spoke out harshly against the White Revolution's reforms. In response, the government sacked the school, killing several students, and arrested Khomeini. He was later exiled, arriving in Turkey, Iraq, and eventually France. During his years of exile, Khomeini stayed in intimate contact with his colleagues in Iran and completed his religio-political doctrine of *velayat-e faqih* (governance by the religious jurist), which provided the theoretical underpinnings for a Shi'ite Islamic state run by the clergy.

Land reform, however, was soon in trouble. The government was unable to put in place a comprehensive support system and infrastructure that replaced the role of the landowner, who had previously provided tenants with all the basic necessities for farming. The result was a high failure rate for new farms and a subsequent flight of agricultural workers and farmers to the country's major cities, particularly Tehran, where a booming construction industry promised employment. The extended family, the traditional support system in Middle Eastern culture, deteriorated as increasing numbers of young Iranians crowded into the country's largest cities, far from home and in search of work, only to be met by high prices, isolation, and poor living conditions.

Domestic reform and industrial development after 1961 were accompanied by an independent national policy in foreign relations, the principles of which were support for the United Nations and peaceful coexistence with Iran's neighbors. The latter of these principles stressed a positive approach in cementing mutually beneficial ties with other countries. Iran played a major role with Turkey and Pakistan in the Central Treaty Organization (CENTO) and Regional Cooperation for Development (RCD). Iran also embarked on trade and cultural relations with France, West Germany, Scandinavia, Eastern Europe, and the Soviet Union.

Relations with the United States remained close, reflected by the increasing predominance of Western culture in the country and the growing number of American advisers, who were necessary to administer the shah's ambitious economic reforms and, most important, to aid in the development of Iran's military. The Iranian army was the cornerstone of the country's foreign policy and had become, thanks to American aid and expertise, the most powerful, well-equipped force in the region and one of the largest armed forces in the world.

World Heritage Sites

Madar-e Shah madrasah
(religious college), Esfahan.

Iran, with its extraordinarily long history, has a huge number of major and minor places of cultural and historical interest. Six of these have been specially recognized by the United Nations Educational, Scientific and Cultural Organization (UNESCO) and have been added to its World Heritage list. Three of the sites—Persepolis, Chogha Zanbil, and the Maydan-e Emam ("Imam's Square") area of Esfahan—were designated in 1979; one—Takht-e Soleyman—in 2003; and two—Pasargadae and the fortress at Bam—in 2004.

Persepolis (Old Persian, Parsa), the ancient capital of the Persian Achaemenian dynasty, is perhaps the best known.

Located about 30 miles northeast of Shiraz in the Fars region of southwestern Iran, the site lies near the confluence of the Sivand and Kor rivers. Construction of the city began under Darius I the Great (reigned 522–486 BC), who made it the capital of Persia proper, replacing Pasargadae. Persepolis was remote, and administration of the empire was carried on from the cities of Susa, Babylon, or Ecbatana. Alexander the Great plundered the city and burned the palace of Xerxes in 330 BC. Persepolis became the capital of the province of Persis in the Macedonian Empire, but the city gradually declined in the Seleucid period and after. Archaeological excavation began in the 19th century, but the major work there took place in the 1930s.

The site consists of a large terrace with its east side abutting the Kuh-e Rahmat ("Mount of Mercy"). The other three sides are formed by a retaining wall; on the west side a double stair in two flights of 111 stone steps leads to the top. On the terrace are the ruins of a number of colossal buildings, all constructed of a dark gray stone quarried from the adjacent mountain. The large and precisely cut stones, many of them still in place, were laid without mortar. Especially striking are 15 extant columns— 13 in the audience hall of Darius I and two more in the entrance hall of the Gate of Xerxes—and another one assembled at the latter site from its broken pieces.

A short distance northeast of Persepolis is Pasargadae, the first Achaemenian capital. Traditionally, Cyrus II the Great (reigned 559–c. 529 BC) chose the site because it lay near the scene of his victory over Astyages the Mede (550). The majestic simplicity of the architecture at Pasargadae reflects a sense of balance and beauty that was never equaled in either earlier or later Achaemenian times. The principal buildings are scattered over a wide area. A strong citadel commands the northern approaches, its dominant feature a huge stone platform projecting from a low, conical hill. Two unfinished stone staircases and a facade of rusticated masonry were evidently intended to form part of an elevated palace enclosure, but a formidable mud-brick structure was erected on the platform instead.

To the south of the citadel was a walled park with gardens surrounded by a series of royal buildings. Structures cleared by modern-day excavations include a tall, square tower; two spacious palaces; and a fourth building designed as the sole entrance to the park. Farther to the south, the tomb of Cyrus still stands almost intact. Constructed of huge, white limestone blocks, its gabled tomb chamber rests on a rectangular, stepped plinth. In Islamic times the tomb acquired new sanctity as the supposed resting place of the mother of King Solomon.

Chogha Zanbil (Tchogha Zanbil) is the ruined palace and temple complex of the ancient Elamite city of Dur Untashi (Dur Untash), near Susa in the Khuzestan region of southwestern Iran. The complex consists of a magnificent ziggurat (the largest of its kind in Iran), temples, and three palaces. Built in about 1250 BC under the Elamite ruler Untash-Gal, the complex was dedicated to Inshushinak (Insusinak), the bull-god of Susa. Its irregularly shaped outer wall extends approximately 3,900 by 2,600 feet around the inner sanctum and 13 temple buildings, of which only four are well preserved. The square base of the ziggurat, 344 feet on each side, was built principally of brick and cement. It now stands 80 feet high, less than half its estimated original height. Its facade was once covered in glazed blue and green terra-cotta, and its interior was decorated in glass and ivory mosaics. At the apex of the building stood a temple from which Inshushinak was believed to ascend to the heavens every night.

Ziggurat at Chogha Zanbil near Susa.

The complex was still unfinished, however, by about 640 BC, when Chogha Zanbil was attacked, looted, and heavily damaged by the Assyrian King Ashurbanipal. Afterward it fell into ruin. It was sighted in 1935 by airplane, and initial studies were performed in the late 1930s; the main excavations were carried out from 1946 to 1962.

Esfahan (Isfahan) is a major city of western Iran. Situated on the north bank of the Zayandeh River, it is roughly 210 miles south of Tehran. In addition to being an important regional and provincial capital, it is one of the most important architectural centers in the Islamic world. The city first thrived under the Seljuq Turks (11th–12th centuries) and then under the Persian Safavid dynasty (16th–18th centuries). Esfahan's golden age began in 1598 when the Safavid ruler 'Abbas I (the Great) made it his capital and rebuilt it into one of the largest and most beautiful cities of the 17th century.

In the center of the city he created the immense Maydan-e Shah ("Royal Square"; former name of the Maydan-e Emam), a courtyard that measures 1,674 by 540 feet. At the southern end of the courtyard is the Masjed-e Shah ("Royal Mosque"; now Masjed-e Emam), begun in 1611–1612 but not finished until after 'Abbas's death. This building, decorated with enameled tiles of great brilliance, has been carefully preserved. On the eastern side stands the Masjed-e Shaykh Lutf Allah ("Sheikh Lotfollah Mosque"), used by 'Abbas for his private devotions. On the western side of the square is the 'Ali Qapu ("Lofty Gate"), a high building in the form of an archway that is crowned in the forepart by an immense covered balcony; it served as an audience hall and as a vantage point from which the shah and his courtiers or guests could watch games of polo or gladiatorial combats below. The archway leads into the gardens of the former royal palace with its courts and pavilions, one of which, the Chehal Sotun ("Forty Columns"), was the veranda and throne room for 'Abbas.

Takht-e Soleyman ("Solomon's Throne") was an ancient city and Zoroastrian temple complex of Iran's Sasanian dynasty (AD 224–651). The site is in northwestern Iran in the southeastern highlands, about 25 miles northeast of the city of Takab. Takht-e Soleyman itself is the center of several groups of ruins (all part of the World Heritage site), which include Zendan-e Soleyman ("Solomon's Prison") and Kuh-e Belqeys ("Mount Belqeys"— Belqeys being the Islamic name for the queen of Sheba), each of which was in some way devoted to Zoroastrian worship. Takht-e Soleyman was established as a Zoroastrian sanctuary in the early to mid-fifth century, when the fire altar Adur Gushnasp—one of the three great Zoroastrian fire altars—was moved there from the Atropatene capital Gazaca (perhaps modern Tabriz). The large, multiroom temple housing the altar is the central building of the Takht-e Soleyman complex, located just inside the complex's northern gate. The buildings at Takht-e Soleyman were originally constructed of mud brick, but large sections of the complex, including the fire temple, were rebuilt of stone and fired bricks in later centuries. The temple complex was sacked and badly damaged by the Byzantines in 623. Following the Islamic conquest, it continued to be used for Zoroastrian worship until perhaps the 10th century, when it was abandoned and fell into ruin.

The town of Bam, in eastern Kerman Province, is about 115 miles southeast of the city of Kerman. It is famous for the Arg-e Bam ("Citadel of Bam"), a fortress located on a hilltop and consisting of a series of three concentric walls made of mud brick and palm timbers. The outer wall enclosed the old town. The fortress's highest point, the citadel proper, rises to about 200 feet above its base. The walls of the fortress are 40 feet in height. The citadel, which dates to Sasanian times, was, even as late as the beginning of the 19th century, the strongest fortified place in Iran. By the late 19th century, however, such a stronghold was obsolete, though the fortress continued to be used as a military garrison until the 1930s. The Iranian government began restoring the fortress in the 1950s, but in 2003 the region around Bam was hit by a massive earthquake that killed as many as 30,000 people and devastated the modern town. The fortress itself was largely destroyed.

Xerxes I

Bas-relief of Xerxes I found at Persepolis.

Xerxes I was a king of the Achaemenian dynasty and ruled Persia from 486 to 465 BC. The son of Darius I, he was the governor of Babylon when his father died and he ascended the throne. In 484, he ferociously suppressed a rebellion in Egypt that his father had sought to quell before his death, and two years later Xerxes quashed an insurrection in Babylonia.

To avenge Darius's defeat by the Greeks at the Battle of Marathon, he spent three years raising a massive army and navy in order to invade Greece. His force eventually numbered, by modern estimates, 360,000 soldiers and 700 ships, which assembled in western Anatolia in 480. When a storm destroyed the bridges he had built to cross the Hellespont into Greece, he had them rebuilt and for seven days oversaw the crossing of his huge army. The enormous Persian force was delayed for three days by a small Spartan-led force at the pass of Thermopylae but soon broke through and pillaged Athens. The subsequent loss of the Persian navy to the Greeks at the Battle of Salamis persuaded Xerxes to withdraw to Asia, but he left behind a large army that withdrew only after its defeat at the Battle of Plataea in 479.

In Persia he began an extensive building campaign at Persepolis. Drawn unwittingly into palace intrigues, he killed his brother's family at the queen's demand. Members of his court then murdered him. His setback in Greece was regarded as the beginning of the decline of the Achaemenian dynasty.

Bibliography

Numerous authors contributed to the material compiled in this work. They include Janet Afary (Purdue University), author of *The Iranian Constitutional Revolution*; Hassan Arfa (Major General, Iranian Army), author of *Under Five Shahs*; Noel James Coulson (University of London), author of *A History of Islamic Law*; Albert L. Danielsen (University of Georgia), author of *The Evolution of OPEC*; Richard N. Frye (Harvard University), author of *The History of Ancient Iran*; Jean-Louis Huot (University of Paris I), author of *Iran*; Karen Mingst (University of Kentucky), author of *Essentials of International Relations* and coauthor of *The United Nations in the Post–Cold War Era*; J. M. Munn-Rankin (University of Cambridge), contributor to *The Cambridge Ancient History*; Roger M. Savory (University of Toronto), translator of *The History of Shah 'Abbas*; and Marilyn R. Waldman (Ohio State University), author of *Toward a Theory of Historical Narrative: A Case Study in Perso-Islamicate Historiography*. For further general information on Iran, see the following: Helen Chapin Metz, ed., *Iran: A Country Study*, 4th ed. (1989), provides a useful overview of all aspects of the country. Ehsan Yarshater, ed., *Encyclopædia Iranica* (1985–), is an extensive reference source.

Land

W. B. Fisher, ed., *The Land of Iran* (1968), vol. 1 of *The Cambridge History of Iran*, is perhaps the single most comprehensive and informative work on geography and social ecology. W. B. Fisher, *The Middle East: A Physical, Social, and Regional Geography*, 7th ed., completely rev. and reset (1978), includes a brief survey of Iran. Also useful are W. Barthold (V. V. Bartold), *An Historical Geography of Iran*, ed. C. E. Bosworth (1984; originally published in Russian, 1903); and the section on Iran in *The Middle East and North Africa* (annual), a country survey with up-to-date statistical data.

People

Jamshid A. Momeni, ed., *The Population of Iran: A Selection of Readings* (1977), covers all aspects of Iran's human resources. Studies of various peoples include Fredrik Barth, *Nomads of South-Persia: The Basseri Tribe of the Khamseh Confederacy* (1961, reissued 1986); Richard Tapper, *Pasture and Politics: Economics, Conflict, and Ritual among Shahsevan Nomads of Northwestern Iran* (1979), an anthropological study; and Lois Beck, *The Qashqa'i of Iran* (1986), a political ethnography. The essays in Richard Tapper, ed., *The Conflict of Tribe and State in Iran and Afghanistan* (1983), assess tribal political and social structures in recent history.

Economy

Charles Issawi, ed., *The Economic History of Iran, 1800–1914* (1971), contains documents, statistical data, and commentary on economic conditions prior to World War I. It may be supplemented by Julian Bharier, *Economic Development in Iran, 1900–1970* (1971), which includes analyses of individual economic sectors; Jahangir Amuzegar, *Iran: An Economic Profile* (1977); and Robert E. Looney, *Economic Origins of the Iranian Revolution* (1982). The important petroleum and natural-gas industries are discussed in M. Froozan, M. Shirazi, and I. Ebtehaj-Sami'i, "The Development of the Gas Industry in Iran," *Tahqiqat-e Eqtesadi: Quarterly Journal of Economic Research* 7 (19–20): 25–47 (Summer and Autumn 1970); and Fereidun Fesharaki, *Development of the Iranian Oil Industry: International and Domestic Aspects* (1976). Agrarian reforms and their impact on rural Iran are detailed in Ann K. S. Lambton, *Landlord and Peasant in Persia* (1953, reissued 1991), and *The Persian Land Reform, 1962–1966* (1969); Eric J. Hooglund, *Land and Revolution in Iran, 1960–1980* (1982); and Afsaneh Najmabadi, *Land Reform and Social Change in Iran* (1987). On Iran's economy since the 1979 revolution, see Saeed Rahnema and Sohrab Behdad, eds., *Iran after the Revolution: Crisis of an Islamic State* (1995).

Government and Society

Useful texts include Marvin Zonis, *The Political Elite of Iran* (1971; reissued 1976); Shahram Chubin and Sepehr Zabih, *The Foreign Relations of Iran: A Developing State in a Zone of Great-Power Conflict* (1974); James A. Bill, *The Eagle and the Lion: The Tragedy of American-Iranian Relations* (1988), a detailed study covering the period from 1835 to the Iran-Contra Affair of 1986–1987; and R. K. Ramazani, *The United States and Iran: The Patterns of Influence* (1982). A. Reza Arasteh, *Education and Social Awakening in Iran, 1850–1968*, 2nd ed. rev. and enlarged (1969), is a critical study of

Iranian education. The interconnections of religion and politics are analyzed by Said Amir Arjomand, *The Shadow of God and the Hidden Imam: Religion, Political Order, and Societal Change in Shi'ite Iran from the Beginning to 1890* (1984; reissued 1987); Nikki R. Keddie, ed., *Religion and Politics in Iran: Shi'ism from Quietism to Revolution* (1983); and Roy Mottahedeh, *The Mantle of the Prophet: Religion and Politics in Iran* (1985; reissued 1987), on the place of religion in 20th-century Iran, set in a historical context. 'Allamah Sayyid Muhammad Husayn Tabataba'i, *Shi'ite Islam*, trans. from Persian by Seyyed Hossein Nasr (1977), provides an authoritative study on the origins and growth of Shi'ism. Works on the religious background of the Islamic revolution of 1979 include Shahrough Akhavi, *Religion and Politics in Contemporary Iran: Clergy-State Relations in the Pahlavi Period* (1980); and Michael M. J. Fisher, *Iran: From Religious Dispute to Revolution* (1980; reprinted 1982). The human rights record of the Islamic republic is discussed in Eliz Sanasarian, *Religious Minorities in Iran* (2000); and Reza Afshari, *Human Rights in Iran: The Abuse of Cultural Relativism* (2001).

Cultural Life

Arthur Upham Pope, *Masterpieces of Persian Art* (1945, reissued 1970); and Hans E. Wulff, *The Traditional Crafts of Persia: Their Development, Technology, and Influence on Eastern and Western Civilizations* (1966; reprinted 1976), are well-documented studies with illustrations. R. W. Ferrier, ed., *The Arts of Persia* (1989), is an extensive, well-illustrated survey covering the Neolithic Period to the 19th century, although it concentrates on Islamic arts. A study of art and literature by Iranian Jews is provided in Houman Sarshar, ed., *Esther's Children: A Portrait of Iranian Jews* (2002). On the Iranian cinema at home and in exile, see Hamid Naficy, *The Making of Exile Cultures: Iranian Television in Los Angeles* (1993).

History

GENERAL WORKS

The Cambridge History of Iran, 7 vol. in 8 (1968–1991), contains extensively documented studies from the beginning to the Safavid period. Essays in volumes of *The Cambridge Ancient History* (1923–1939), some volumes available in later editions, also examine particular periods. Single-volume works include Percy Sykes, *A History of Persia*, 3rd ed., 2 vols. (1930, reissued 1969); R. Ghirshman,

Iran: From the Earliest Times to the Islamic Conquest (1954, reissued 1978); Alessandro Bausani, *The Persians: From the Earliest Days to the Twentieth Century* (1971; reprinted 1975; originally published in Italian, 1962); Richard N. Frye, *The Heritage of Persia*, corrected 2nd ed. (1976; reprinted 1993), and *The History of Ancient Iran* (1984); and Donald N. Wilber, *Iran, Past and Present: From Monarchy to Islamic Republic*, 9th ed. (1981). Dynastic tables and essays on different aspects of Iranian history and culture may be found in A. J. Arberry, ed., *The Legacy of Persia* (1953, reissued 1968).

IRAN FROM 640 TO C. 1500

Modern research has produced articles on Iran in P. M. Holt, Ann K. S. Lambton, and Bernard Lewis, eds., *The Cambridge History of Islam*, 2 vols. (1970, reissued in 4 vols., 1980). An essential reference work is *The Encyclopaedia of Islam*, 4 vols. and supplement (1913–1938); a new ed. (1960–2005). W. Barthold (V. V. Bartold), *Turkestan down to the Mongol Invasion*, 4th ed. (1977; originally published in Russian, 2 vols. in 1, 1898–1900), is the essential survey of northeastern Iranian history from about AD 600 to the 13th century. Iran under Arab governors in the seventh to ninth centuries is explored in Richard N. Frye, *The Golden Age of Persia: The Arabs in the East* (1975; reprinted 1996). M. A. Shaban, *The 'Abbasid Revolution* (1970; reissued 1979), concentrates on the Arab conquest and settlement of Khorasan. Discussions of various ruling dynasties of the period between the end of the 'Abbasid Empire and the rise of the Seljuqs may be found in Clifford Edmund Bosworth, *The Ghaznavids: Their Empire in Afghanistan and Eastern Iran, 994–1040*, 2nd ed. (1973; reissued 1992), and *The Later Ghaznavids: Splendour and Decay* (1977; reissued 1992); and Roy P. Mottahedeh, *Loyalty and Leadership in an Early Islamic Society* (1980), on the Buyids, their subjects, and their social structure. The Seljuqs and Mongols are the subjects of Ann K. S. Lambton, *Continuity and Change in Medieval Persia: Aspects of Administrative, Economic, and Social History, 11th–14th Century* (1988); and David Morgan, *The Mongols* (1986; reissued 1992), and *Medieval Persia, 1040–1797* (1988), which covers events up to the Qajar period.

IRAN FROM C. 1500 TO C. 1950

Roger Savory, *Iran under the Safavids* (1980), surveys the rise and fall of the Safavid dynasty; and Charles Melville, ed., *Safavid Persia: The History of and Politics of an Islamic Society* (1996), explores many religious, cultural, and economic issues of that period. The brief Zand dynasty is examined by John R. Perry, *Karim Khan Zand: A History of Iran, 1747–1779* (1979). Studies of the Qajar period may be found in Firuz Kazemzadeh, *Russia and Britain in Persia, 1864–1914: A Study in Imperialism* (1968); Ann K. S. Lambton, *Qajar Persia: Eleven Studies* (1987), a collection of previously published essays on agriculture and commerce in 19th-century Iran; and Clifford Edmund Bosworth and Carole Hillenbrand, eds., *Qajar Iran: Political, Social, and Cultural Change, 1800–1925* (1983; reissued 1992). Hamid Algar, *Religion and State in Iran, 1785–1906: The Role of the 'Ulama' in the Qajar Period* (1969, reissued 1980); and Mangol Bayat, *Mysticism and Dissent: Socioreligious Thought in Qajar Iran* (1982), discuss 19th-century religious development. The economic changes of the 19th and early 20th centuries are discussed by John Foran, *Fragile Resistance: Social Transformation in Iran from 1500 to the Revolution* (1993). Works on the Constitutional Revolution include Janet Afary, *The Iranian Constitutional Revolution, 1906–1911: Grassroots Democracy, Social Democracy & the Origins of Feminism* (1996); Mangol Bayat, *Iran's First Revolution: Shi'ism and the Constitutional Revolution of 1905–1909* (1991); Edward G. Browne, *The Persian Revolution of 1905–1909*, new ed., ed. Abbas Amanat (1995); and Vanessa Martin, *Islam and Modernism: The Iranian Revolution of 1906* (1989). M. Reza Ghods, *Iran in the Twentieth Century: A Political History* (1989), is also useful. Works on the period of the Pahlavi dynasty include Ervand Abrahamian, *Iran between Two Revolutions* (1982), covering 1905 to 1979; and Fakhreddin Azimi, *Iran: The Crisis of Democracy* (1989).

IRAN SINCE C. 1950

The political and socioeconomic background of the Islamic revolution is explored by Nikki R. Keddie and Yann Richard, *Roots of Revolution: An Interpretive History of Modern Iran* (1981); Mohsen M. Milani, *The Making of Iran's Islamic Revolution: From Monarchy to Islamic Republic*, 2nd ed. (1994); Mohammed Amjad, *Iran: From Royal Dictatorship to Theocracy* (1989); Misagh Parsa, *Social Origins of the Iranian Revolution* (1989); and Habib Ladjevardi, *Labor Unions and Autocracy in Iran* (1985). Information on the religious background of the revolution can be found in Said Amir Arjomand, *The Shadow of God and the Hidden Imam: Religion, Political Order, and Societal Change in Shi'ite Iran from the Beginning to 1890* (1984, reissued 1987), and *The Turban for the Crown: The Islamic Revolution in Iran* (1988); Nikki R. Keddie, ed., *Religion and Politics in Iran: Shi'ism from*

Quietism to Revolution (1983); and Roy Mottahedeh, *The Mantle of the Prophet: Religion and Politics in Iran* (1985, reissued 1987), on the place of religion in 20th-century Iran, set in a historical context. The Islamic republic itself is the subject of Shaul Bakhash, *The Reign of the Ayatollahs: Iran and the Islamic Revolution*, rev. ed. (1990); Robin Wright, *Sacred Rage: The Crusade of Modern Islam* (1985), and *In the Name of God: The Khomeini Decade* (1989, reissued 1991), which recount Iran's efforts to export its revolution to other Islamic countries; and R. K. Ramazani, *Revolutionary Iran: Challenge and Response in the Middle East* (1986, reissued 1988 with a new epilogue on the Iranian-American arms deal). The war in the Persian Gulf between Iran and Iraq is analyzed by several prearmistice works, such as Shahram Chubin and Charles Tripp, *Iran and Iraq at War* (1988, reissued 1991); Majid Khadduri, *The Gulf War: The Origins and Implications of the Iraq-Iran Conflict* (1988); and Edgar O'Ballance, *The Gulf War* (1988), a narrative of military operations; and by several postarmistice publications, including Hanns W. Maull and Otto Pick, eds., *The Gulf War: Regional and International Dimensions* (1989); and Efraim Karsh, ed., *The Iran-Iraq War: Impact and Implications* (1989). On the history of the Iranian women's movement, see Eliz Sanasarian, *The Women's Rights Movement in Iran: Mutiny, Appeasement, and Repression from 1900 to Khomeini* (1982); and Parvin Paidar, *Women and the Political Process in Twentieth-Century Iran* (1995).